Lingerie

A Lexicon Of Style

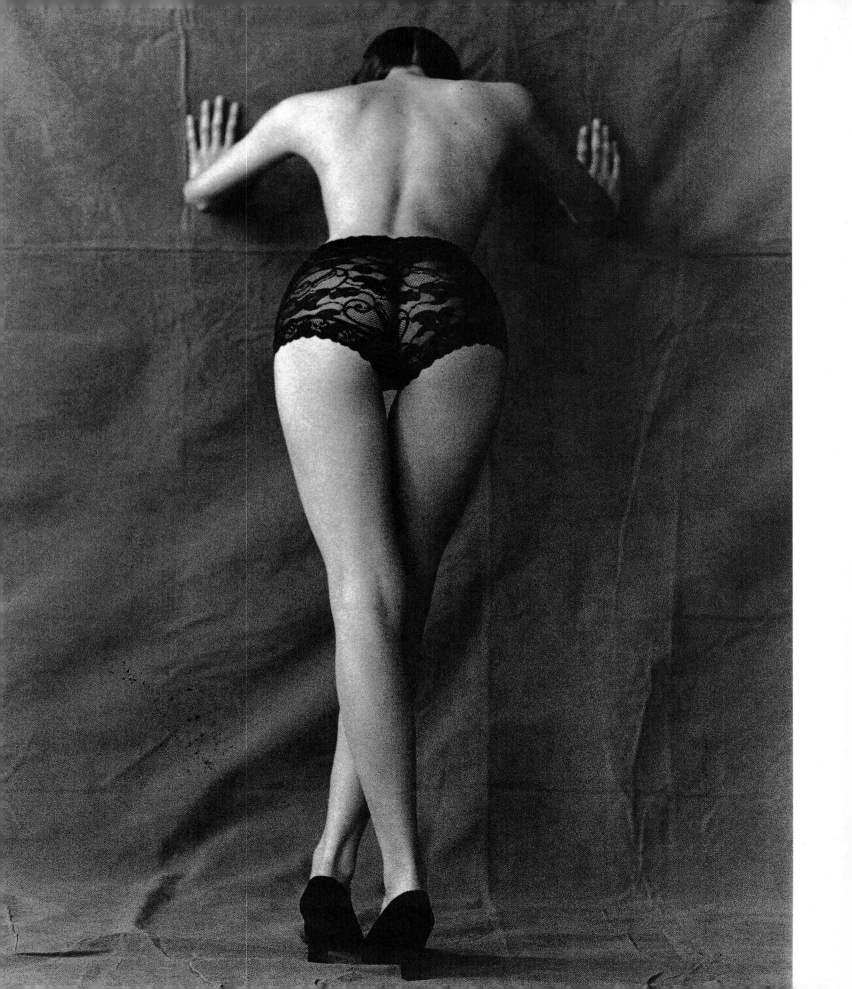

Lingerie

A LEXICON OF STYLE

WRITTEN BY CAROLINE COX

SCRIPTUM EDITIONS
LONDON · HONG KONG

Publisher *Beatrice Vincenzini*

Executive Director *David Shannon*

Editorial Director *Alexandra Black*

Art Director *David Mackintosh*

Publishing Assistant *Mitzi Friedberg*

Picture Researcher *Dinny Gollop*

Studio Photographer *Fred Corcoran*

First published in the UK by Scriptum Editions

Created by Co & Bear Productions (UK) Ltd.

Printed and bound in Novara, Italy by Officine Grafiche de Agostini.

First edition

10 9 8 7 6 5 4 3 2 1

ISBN 1-902686-08-X

Photographs: page 2 Shane Martin for Collette Dinnigan;

This page: courtesy Jean Claude Jitrois;

Overleaf: illustration by Tanya Ling

CONTENTS

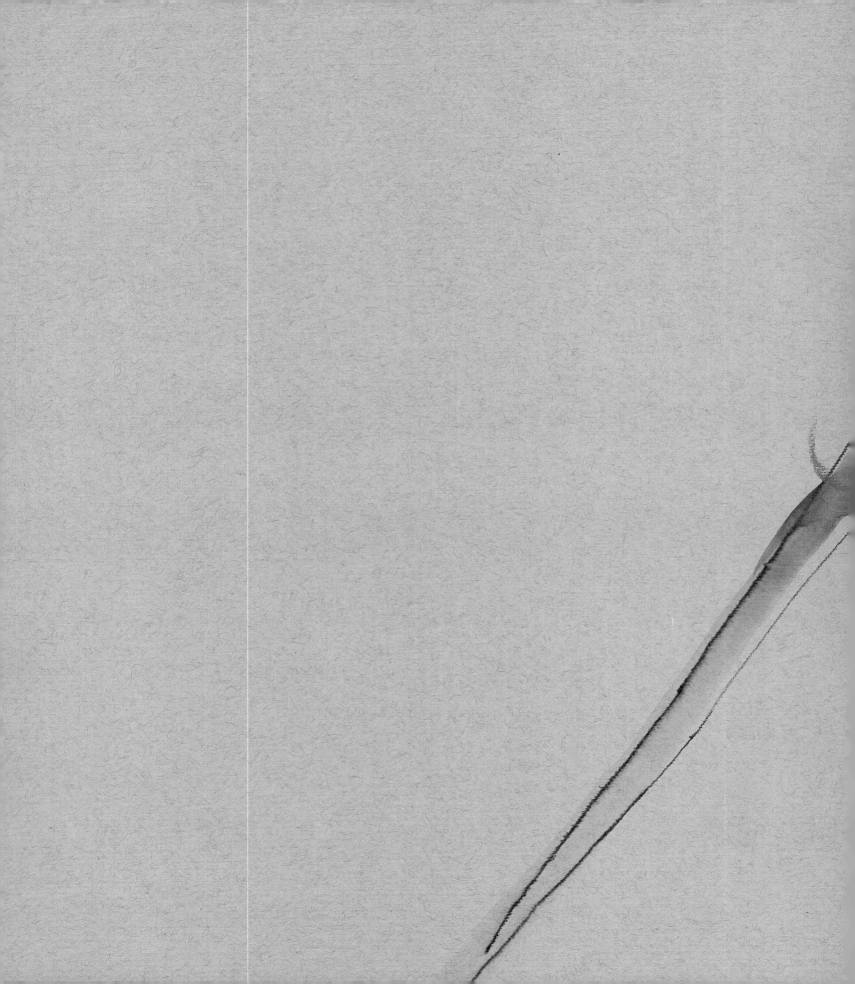

introduction

"Without foundations there can be no fashion."[1]

Christian Dior

Underwear is both mute and meaningful. Initially functional, by the twenty-first century it calls like a siren to the erotic sensibilities of wearer and spectator by both concealing and revealing our most intimate parts. There is an inherent tension in underwear. We are fascinated by what others may be wearing next to their skin but repulsed by traces of the body left behind. We enter its private domain to choose sensual silks and satins that we assume will be seen, but we never "wash our dirty linen in public," as the saying goes. Underwear is there to disguise the messy reality of the body's function. One of the first pieces of advice we are ever given is to wear clean underwear every day, for fear of being run over by a bus and having to go to hospital where the secret of our drawers will be publicly displayed. In matters of underwear, then, it is important to be vigilant at all times. Why else would we refer to certain items in the underwear repertoire as "unmentionables"?

That underwear is primarily worn for modesty's sake is made clear in the biblical case of Adam and Eve. Becoming aware of their naked state, and thus their worldliness, in the Garden of Eden, they hide their genitals with fig leaves. But the double meaning of underwear is also clear in this story – although ostensibly there to cover up, in doing so it acts as a sexual signal, drawing attention to our intimate organs. The bra, for example, allows the breasts to mimic the buttocks, and the penis sheaths of New Guinea or the fifteenth-century codpiece bestow a virile sexual power on the male. Thus the beauty of underwear acts as a signal or even substitute for the beauty of the body, and in the case of fetishism becomes the sexual object itself. Underwear makes

ABOVE This Roxy Music album cover – with its models playing peek-a-boo – comments with wit on the modesty of underwear. The transparency of the garments conceals yet reveals the women's bodies; the lace of their panties gently references pubic hair which is visually reinforced by the background vegetation.

particular areas of the body mysterious and compelling, by hiding them, for as is well known, concealment provides food for our inquisitive natures. Hiding our private parts also serves to hide our desires. As the psychologist Alexander Lowen has pointed out: "The genital organs are covered because their reactions are least subject to voluntary control. While we can mask certain feelings or prevent them from showing in our faces, we can be betrayed by a genital excitation that cannot be controlled. Pride informs a man that his sense of privacy requires that his sexual feelings be kept hidden from public view."[2] Thus the wearing of underwear prevents what the anthropologist Ted Polhemus calls "erotic seepage"[3] in public encounters, thereby helping us to maintain our "highly public presentation of self."[4]

The first items in the underwear wardrobe were linen shifts, described by Richard Martin, Curator of Costume at the Metropolitan Museum of Art in New York, as garments "one step removed from the fig leaf."[5] Their function was to protect the more expensive outer garments from the dirt of the body beneath in times when bathing was a luxury, as well as to provide an extra layer of insulation. However, by the nineteenth century the meanings of underwear were located firmly within the realm of the erotic, and certain garments began to fulfill a pivotal role in pornography and general titillation. Underwear was also contributing to the definition of male and female identities, and the gender roles that went with them, by helping to construct the general silhouette of fashion. From corsets to crinolines and bustles, underwear became a kind of exo-skeleton, marking out fashionable men and women from their peers.

Color and material have also played their parts in the development of underwear – white for the bride's trousseau to represent the virgin state, red for a more raunchy look. Marks & Spencer cotton undies may be worn for every-day, but swapped for a little something in silk from La Perla at night. But it is Lycra that has caused the biggest changes in the look, feel, and function of underwear. With its powerful restraining effects it has made bones, hooks, eyes, and zips redundant, improving fit, cost, and most importantly comfort.

Do we wear expensive undies for our own narcissistic pleasure or for the intimate gaze of our partner? This is a moot point. Many would say that women's underwear in particular is worn for the pleasure and privilege of the male gaze – all those unwanted, scratchy garter belts given at Christmas, only to be exchanged for something a bit more functional after the festivities are over. With the advent of Calvin Klein underpants for men, however, one could say that pleasure in looking is now crossing genders. It should also be noted that the rise of women in the executive arena during the 1980s was accompan-ied by a corresponding boom in the sale of women's underwear. Fancy under-garments have become the mark of a successful career woman rather than a kept mistress – just see Demi Moore get her kit off in *Disclosure*, slipping out of a power suit to reveal a lacy teddy with stockings. These are not items worn by malleable sex objects. The rise in this market has led fashion designers to create their own ranges with a new array of labels conferring cult status.

ABOVE British designer Liza Bruce uses unconventional materials associated with the fetish underground to create new forms of underwear for the confident woman in control.

OPPOSITE The toned, taut, tanned body – a product of late twentieth-century gym culture – is displayed in an eye-catching bra and briefs set by Ann Summers that treads a fine line between sex appeal and sportiness.

Traditional underwear suppliers such as Marks & Spencer have responded in kind by repositioning themselves in an increasingly crowded marketplace, as have Rigby & Peller, bespoke corsetieres to H.M. Queen Elizabeth II and the Queen Mother. This company, first established in 1939, is now one of the main players in the luxury underwear market – their shop assistants are reputedly able to tell a customer's bust size at a glance.

In this book the many layers of underwear meaning are uncovered. Chapter one traces the development of the corset, from function to fetish to fashion-as-outerwear by the late twentieth century. Whether this garment is an agent of women's oppression is still source for debate in popular culture, but it is clear that many women feel a sense of power dressing up in something so overtly sexual. Chapter two investigates the relationship between the aesthetics of the breasts and their container – the bra. Chapter three looks at the most functional of undergarments, underpants. Whatever we call them – pants, knickers, drawers, briefs – they tread an uneasy path between utility and fantasy, and can easily turn our thoughts toward jokes about "gussets" or scenes from low comedy. Chapters four and five look at two of the more specialist areas of the underwear market – bedroom lingerie and its polar opposite, sports underwear.

According to cultural historian Valerie Steele, the debates over the origins and function of underwear all have ideas about sexuality at their root: "As Freud says, 'At the root of every taboo, there must be a desire.' When desires are repressed, people feel ambivalent. What could be a more ambivalent symbol than the fig leaf, calling attention to that which it ostensibly hides?"[6]

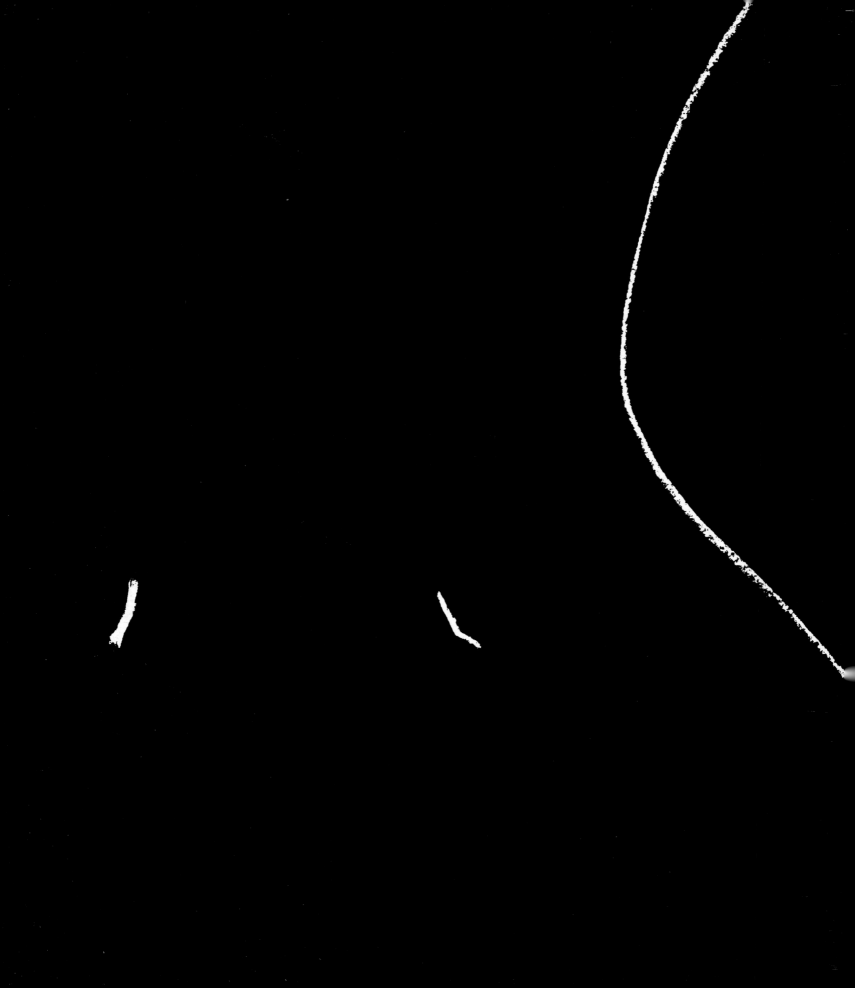

chapter one Waisted Wear

waisted wear

"Le corset, c'est une chose orthopédique."[1]

Madeleine Vionnet

ABOVE To many Victorians, both the mirror and the corset symbolized women's self-absorption and vanity – the consequences of which were frivolous female fashions.

OPPOSITE Helmut Newton captures the woman as sexual dominatrix, this time flashing her black Wolford "body" with matching sheer hold-ups. Dark glasses help retain her anonymity.

On 11 March 1999, *Vogue Daily* described the latest collection of British fashion designer Alexander McQueen as "a cold, lifeless production line of blank-faced models with crimped Replicant bobs ... wearing hi-tech white-on-black circuit board print catsuits, cream android dresses hung from silver shoulders, and see-through Plexiglass microchip corsets flashing with miniature bulbs and metal wires."[2] In the midst of a culture dominated by visions of a dystopian future and the impact of new technology, McQueen is still renegotiating that most ubiquitous of garments, the corset. In this he resembles many other late twentieth-century designers: Tristan Webber shows delicate patchwork corsets in chestnut, cream, and burgundy leather; Dolce & Gabbana uses rubber; Jean-Paul Gaultier prefers a worn denim version; and Lolita Lempicka supplies a vision of saloon girls dressed in corsets, complete with rosebud corsages. Once private, the corset can now be both underwear and outerwear in the theater of fashion. The corset wearer can no longer be dubbed a fashion victim, as the garment invokes sexual power rather than submission.

The original corset is said by fashion historians to derive from the "cotte" of the 1300s. A rigid laced tunic of linen, stiffened with paste to fit closely to the body, the cotte helped create the slim, serpentine silhouette of medieval Europe. When the front and back parts of the cotte were laced together, it eventually evolved into the corset.

In the eighteenth century, the corset became a device that compressed the waist, thereby drawing sexual attention to the bust and hips by creating the hourglass figure. It was then that corsets began to attract a more negative kind

of interest due to their association with the conspicuous licentious-ness of the French aristocracy. The corset was an obvious sexualiz-ing device, as its compression of the diaphragm led to shallow breathing in the upper half of the body, both causing and drawing attention to the "heaving bosoms" so popular in romantic fiction.

This libidinous, luxuriant style of corset wearing was an inspir-ation for the British fashion designer Vivienne Westwood in her seminal Portrait Collection (1990). This featured photographically printed corsets, using designs directly lifted from the work of the French Rococo painter François Boucher (1703–70).

The style of the eighteenth-century corset copied by Westwood, squeezing the breasts from below to make them bulge upwards and out, was originally associated with a leisured femininity. The corset's restriction of move-ment made physical labor out of the question, so to wear a tightly laced corset was a mark of social status and success for a woman, while also displaying the wealth of the man who could support such an ornament as a wife.

As Thorstein Veblen commented in his famous essay *The Theory of the Leisure Class*, first published in 1899: "The high heel, the skirt, the impractic-able bonnet, the corset, and the general disregard of the wearer's comfort which is an obvious feature of all civilized women's apparel, are so many items of evidence to the effect that in the modern civilized scheme of life the woman is still, in theory, the economic dependant of the man, that, perhaps in a highly idealized sense, she is still the man's chattel."[3]

ABOVE All manner of eccentric devices were invented in the nineteenth century to aid women in their quest for the perfect shape. The Harness electric corset was one of many mechanical versions which entered this potentially lucrative market, using the wonders of the new electricity to give the corset a quasi-scientific, and thus more convincing, bent in 1891.

In the late twentieth century, however, Vivienne Westwood cheekily subverted all these notions through the use of new materials such as Lycra, rather than the original whalebone or steel stays, creating a look that was easy to wear either in the bedroom or the boardroom. She complained that: "For the last ten years clothes have had shoulder pads and tight hips – that's supposed to be the sexy look, the inverted triangle – but I think people want a more feminine fitting. Women want to be strong but in a feminine way."[4] This was a new kind of power dressing for the urban working woman, shown to its most dramatic effect in her Stature of Liberty corset of 1987. This was the ultimate in "corset comfort" – two words that in the past would never have been seen together. The elasticized sides of the Westwood corset meant an end to laces at the front or back. The garment could be pulled over the head and then over the body in one easy movement.

Before the twentieth century, corsets were not just there for fashion. They were also believed to lend support to the supposedly structurally unsound, fragile bodies of women and children, as well as to their easily besieged morality. Comments upon a woman's sexuality could be made through her corset: she was either "strait-laced" or "loose." A popular *mise en scène* was that of the cuckolded husband discovering his wife's infidelity because the knots in her corset laces were different from the ones he had studiously tied that morning. A solution for the wayward wife came with the invention of the mechanical corset, displayed at the Exposition Universelle in Paris in 1823. This understructure had an arrangement of small pulleys that enabled women to lace up their own corsets without the aid of a maid or lover. It did not catch on.

The unlacing of a corset was a calibration of a lover's expertise, as the journalist Michael Bywater explains: "How many experienced women had carefully fumbled with a button to give the impression of trembling ingenuousness? How many men had detected prior adventures when too-skilled fingers plied their prestidigitations, and, at once, converted a prospective engagement into a stringless fling? How many women had yielded, feeling in safe hands, by the calm ease with which an older gentleman had negotiated her bows and hooks and buttons?"[5]

The most important effect of the corset was aesthetic, emphasizing a tiny waist above a voluminous crinoline – think of Hollywood's re-interpretation with Scarlett O'Hara in *Gone With the Wind* or Deborah Kerr in *The King and I*. But its erotic appeal was not limited to the waist. According to one writer, corsets also made the breasts "majestic protuberances, pale and soft, as though two pears gathered in a pair of goblets."[6] To achieve this result, by the end of the nineteenth century there was a corset for every occasion, as corset historian Beatrice Fontanel demonstrates:

> *Catalogs offered a wide selection: nuptial corsets, corsets made of white satin for the ball, lightly boned morning corsets, stayless corsets for nightwear, nursing corsets with drawbridge gussets, traveling corsets with*

OPPOSITE H. Sherwood & Co's advertisement of 1898 for the "Elegante" corset. It displays the ideal shape that the product purported to achieve for the wearer. It is the fantastic body shape in illustrations such as this that has helped to maintain the myth of the tiny Victorian waist.

OPPOSITE One of the earliest instances of underwear as outer-wear. The Bunny Girl corset was a weapon to be wielded in a conventionally subservient role as waitress. The Bunny had the last laugh over her male customers as she had one of the most lucrative jobs for women in the immediate post-war years.

tabs that could be let out at night for sleeping, riding corsets with elastic at the hips; corsets for singing, for dancing, for bathing at the seaside (unboned), for riding the velocipede (made of jersey); cool and supple doeskin corsets for summer wear, pearl gray or chamois-colored and trimmed with nile or periwinkle satin; and net corsets of violet silk cord with a small sachet of perfume hanging in the center.[7]

Corsets had been ridiculed and castigated before the nineteenth century, but it was in that century when the complaints began in earnest. Urban folktales abounded of tightly laced corsets deforming the body, displacing internal organs and even cutting livers in half. An article that appeared in a Parisian newspaper in 1859 read: "A young woman, whose thin waist was admired by all her rivals, died two days after the ball. What had happened? Her family decided to find out the cause of her sudden death at such a young age and had an autopsy performed. The findings were rather surprising; the liver had been pierced by three of the girl's ribs! This shows how one may die at the age of twenty-three, not of typhus or in childbirth but because of a corset."[8]

Moralizers, usually conservative men, leapt on the anti-corset bandwagon. In 1857 Charles Dubois published a book entitled *An Examination of Five Plagues: Corsets, Tobacco, Gambling, Strong Drink and Illegal Speculation.* Medical evidence was used to bolster the anti-corset arguments. But what were the castigators of the corset really worried about? As costume historians such as Alison Carter[9] and Valerie Steele[10] have argued, most of the horror stories

OPPOSITE There is precious little ambiguity here as Tim Curry

– in h s seminal role as the voracious Frank 'n' Furter in *The Rocky*

Horror Picture Show – takes the taboo of transvestism mainstream

by strutting his stuff in corset, fishnets, and pearls.

regarding the corset were grossly exaggerated and distorted. Women's waists were never really that small. The popular notion that some Victorian women went to the lengths of having ribs removed to create a tiny waist is a myth.

BELOW Moschino's corset design plays on the sexualized undergarments of the courtesan, juxtaposing scarlet satin, luxurious lace, sheer stockings, and fabulous jewelry.

David Kunzle has made the case for the complaints stemming from a worry that women, by tightly lacing their corsets, were rejecting the maternal role ascribed to them. For what does the corset do but emphasize a woman's waist, the first curve to disappear during pregnancy, thus challenging the virility of men, who had failed in their task to impregnate. It was even mooted that the corset could act as an abortificant if laced tightly enough. Kunzle points out that most of the myths surrounding the corset came from the mouths of nineteenth-century reformers who feared tightlacers could be go-getting young women, freeing themselves from their reproductive role by indulging in the latest fashions. The corset, he believes, was a kind of body armor: "It is as if woman puts it over her vulnerable womanhood, which is however, preserved – indeed exaggerated – beneath. This very act of hardening and stiffening

herself, which is on one level defensive, becomes a militant form of transference to herself of masculine eroticism."[11] The hardness of the outer shell of the corset acts as a defensive shield over the innate softness of the woman's body and suggests references to military might and masculinity. These associations were brought to the fore in the late 1990s as women with Joan of Arc haircuts and gym-hardened bodies wore corset-inspired tops in combination with

OPPOSITE The airplane as a place of erotic encounter features in many sexual fantasies. The imagery used by Knickerbox invokes shades of the "Mile High Club" with the air hostess, a staple of soft pornography, stripped off and ready for action.

combat trousers and Buffalo trainers, a look that displayed a militant strength rather than feminine passivity.

And of course corsetry is not just for the shaping of women's bodies; some men have regularly worn a form of corset for support and control, not to mention fetishistic ritual, which is where the vogue for tight lacing really originated. Dandies of the 1820s – looking uncannily like Mr Pearl, famed for his wasp waist and corsetiere skills in the 1990s – wore boned back-tied corsets to achieve a perfect figure. The purpose of early nineteenth-century men's corsetry, initiated by figures such as Beau Brummell (1778–1840), was to achieve a wasp waist in order to exaggerate a manly chest. Jean-Paul Gaultier's experiments with corsets for men in the 1980s and 1990s have achieved similar effects.

Corsets have also been a perennial favorite of transvestites, as they can instantly create a curvy feminine line without the use of awkward padding. Corsets often play a starring role in cross-dressing fiction, particularly the popular transvestite fantasy of being forced as a man to wear a tightly laced corset under a frilly frock. Firms such as Romantasy sell 40 percent of their custom-made corsets to men. Misty, a transvestite corset enthusiast, describes wearing a corset "under my business clothes and even out on weekends. It is even possible, with some adjustments, to wear your corset all the time. The only comments I receive are how great my posture is. I just say, 'I'm wearing a back brace.' "[12]

It is the nineteenth-century negativity about the garment that informed responses to the corset by feminists in the 1970s and 1980s. Some feminist writers, such as Susan Faludi[13] and Helene Roberts,[14] have regarded the corset as a

symbol of the oppression of women under patriarchy and the sheer agony of fashion blindly followed by its compliant victims. However, one could argue that the twentieth-century cult of the slender body is far more oppressive than corsetry. The fashionable body has to be achieved these days through a far more rigorous system of body maintenance, a "corset of muscle" as the cultural historian Elizabeth Wilson puts it,[15] and the wearing of any body-shaping garment is seen as cheating. A corset can be put on and taken off at will – after a night of tightlacing, a woman can let it all hang out until the next time. But with "natural" body shaping, a woman has to be vigilant at all times and cannot use external substitutes for diet and exercise – it is all about mental discipline. So are corsets really that bad?

On the back of the dress reform movement in the early twentieth century, fashion designers such as Paul Poiret declared the corset dead. Yet it was to resurface in different forms and contexts. In the 1920s, for example, the role of constricting the body into the desired form was taken by the dancing or sports corset – what became known as the corselette or girdle. Made by firms such as Berlei, it was essential for the flapper who wanted to tango. Slimness was also acquired by body maintenance. Dieting began to be promoted by high fashion magazines such as *Vogue*, which in 1922 asked: "With the aid of the corsetiere, the physical culturist and the non-starchy diet, shall we soon develop a race of slender, willowy women? After all, how much more enjoyment can one get out of life if one is slim and active, and excess of avoirdupois leads to inactivity and boredom. Long live the mode of slimness." By the 1940s beauty writers were

OPPOSITE Decked out in her black corset, this powerful *femme fatale* disavows any hint of compliancy or sexual passivity with her stance and gaze. Illustration by Tanya Ling.

OVERLEAF Tiny hands pull the laces of a magical corset that transforms a gigantic female body into an idealized hourglass shape. Unrestrained female flesh bulges from the sides of this comically delicate lace version. Illustration by Richard Gray.

advising their readers that "there is no such thing as a 'stylish stout.' Stoutness is forever unhealthy, unstylish, and unnecessary. If you have allowed yourself to become overweight, get your waistline down again. Flatten it. Strengthen it. Make it your aim in life to keep your muscles so strong and elastic that you can free yourself permanently from that one-piece harness called the corset. Your own muscular corset is the best of all undergarments."[16] Following this kind of advice, some unfortunate women even resorted to rubber "reducing corsets" to sweat off their excess weight.

Lastex or elasticized models of corset, developed by the Dunlop Rubber Company, reigned throughout the 1940s and 1950s. They had the important capacity for two-way stretch, and were called "roll-ons" because that it is what you had to do to get them on. One particularly fraught night during the London Blitz in the Second World War, my grandmother, Marjorie Sartory, was terrified when, in the midst of an explosion, she was suddenly jerked violently backwards into a door. At first she thought the house had sustained a direct hit, but then she realized that the back of her elasticized roll-on had caught on the door handle and, as she rushed past, had pulled her back like a giant catapult.

The girdle appeared in a more glamorous, romanticized form with Christian Dior's Corolle line, or "New Look" as it was dubbed by the press. Using ideas developed by Marcel Rochas in 1945, Dior squeezed his mannequins into "waist cinchers" or "waspies," belt-like corsets that reduced the waist, accompanied by large bell-shaped skirts that harked back to the nineteenth century. *Picture Post* magazine deemed this look unsuitable for the woman who had been working during the war: "Paris forgets this is 1947. There can be no question about the entire unsuitability of these new fashions for our present life and times. Think of doing housework, or sitting at a type-writer all day, or working in a factory, tightly corseted and encumbered and constricted with layers of hip padding and petticoats. Our mothers freed us from these in their struggle for emancipation and in our own active, workaday lives there can be no place for them." However, women liked these glamorous body-shaping devices and fashion designers competed to create various types of "stays" for evening wear. Hardy Amies came up with the evocative titles of "Charade" and "Pink Champagne" for his styles.

It was in the 1950s that corsetry began to be associated with fuddy-duddy adults. Young women were unwilling to put up with undergarments that were too confining. Enter the combination of bra and panty girdle, for to be able to bend at the waist was essential for jiving. Wholesale corsetry went into decline and manufacturers such as Symingtons and Spirella went out of business, as did the majority of corset retailers. At the same time, the corset began to go underground, appearing as a central component of the fetishist's wardrobe. As Valerie Steele noted in her book *Fetish: Fashion, Sex and Power*: "The corset, like the shoe, was one of the first items of clothing to be treated as a fetish, and it remains one of the most important fetish fashions."[17]

Freud describes a fetish object such as the corset as a substitute for the mother's penis, which has been found

missing by the male child during his early sexual development. The lack of his mother's penis engenders a fear of castration in the child that can only be eased with a penis substitute, that is, the fetish object. As Freud states: "The fetish is a substitute for the woman's (the mother's) penis that the little boy once believed in and does not want to give up."[18] Thus as Louise Kaplan suggests: "The adult fetishist cannot introduce his penis into that temple of doom called a vagina without a fetish to ease the way."[19] But why should tightly laced corsets be so popular in the fetish underworld? Freud believed it was related to the child's memories of the mother undressing before the realization of castration: "Pieces of underclothing, which are so often chosen as a fetish, crystallize the moment of undressing, the last moment in which the woman could still be regarded as phallic."[20]

The rites of initiation into the forbidden mysteries of adult sexuality through an eroticized corset are evocatively described by French author Marcel Aymé in the novel *La Jument Verte*:

> On Sunday morning, Frederic and Antoine would rise early and post themselves at one of the small round windows to watch the policeman's wife, bare-armed and wearing a pink corset, open the blinds on the other side of the street. Her enormous arms had the livid hue and bright pink marbling one finds on pigs' bellies. Tufts of black hair poked out from the

ABOVE LEFT & RIGHT Two examples of nineteenth-century corsetry show details of the intricate construction, boning, and lacing techniques which once achieved the fashionable figure.

OPPOSITE In the twentieth century the corset reappears as a fetish object – the laces pierce the eyelets, mimicking sexual intercourse. This boned ribbon waist cincher is a contemporary design from Sh!, the London sex emporium for women.

OPPOSITE Nina Ricci's corset design in white lace harks
back to one of the golden ages of underwear, the 1950s,
creating a soft-focus nostalgic look.

BELOW In the late twentieth century Madonna redefined
the corset, changing its status from intimate underwear to
sassy, confrontational outerwear. This image of her for the
album *Like a Virgin* has achieved iconic status.

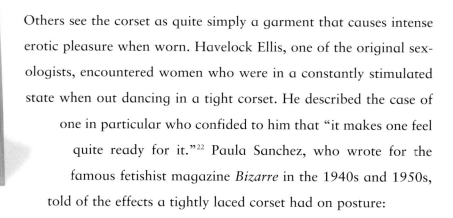

*short sleeves of her shirt. Casting a glance into the street, she leaned
with both hands against the window ledge, making deep folds appear
by her armpits, as great as buttock creases. What most caught the boys'
fancy was the pink corset. You could not see what was inside, as it
fitted over a barely open shirt. But within its projections, its resurgences,
lapped in whalebone and pink fabric, the two brothers imagined a
molten and voluptuous flood of mysteries, an agglutination beyond
the bounds of geometry, an inexhaustible font of femininity,
rolling in a fug of sweat and milking parlors.[21]*

Others see the corset as quite simply a garment that causes intense
erotic pleasure when worn. Havelock Ellis, one of the original sex-
ologists, encountered women who were in a constantly stimulated
state when out dancing in a tight corset. He described the case of
one in particular who confided to him that "it makes one feel
quite ready for it."[22] Paula Sanchez, who wrote for the
famous fetishist magazine *Bizarre* in the 1940s and 1950s,
told of the effects a tightly laced corset had on posture:

*When high heels are worn with the hourglass corset that is properly laced,
walking produces an indescribably interesting movement of both breast
and hips which cannot in any way be compared to the effects of the
present bra and hip girdle. The slight jar produced by extra high heels*

OPPOSITE Basia Zarzycka, a designer who plays with the notion of the corset as outerwear rather than underwear, uses fine detailing of beads and embroidery to create a garment intended for public display rather than intimacy.

results in an eye-catching quivering wave in the plump protruding breasts, which alternately press out and fall back into the corset almost vertically. There is an alternate side to side movement of the hips, a sway in the direction of whichever foot happens to be carrying the weight. With a tightly constricted waist and very high heels this hula-like movement becomes automatic with every step and the tighter the corset, the more emphatic becomes this movement of the derriere.[23]

Other advocates of the tightly laced corset take their fantasies to extremes, preaching the exquisite torture of extreme body modification and the discipline needed in order to accomplish it successfully. As fetishist Mr Pearl says: "[It's] about control of yourself [and] brings with it certain rules; you can't do certain things. You can't slouch. If I don't put a corset on it doesn't feel right. I sleep in my corset, or in a belt, because it's best to feel it always being controlled. It makes me feel better."[24]

Ethel Granger, who in her lifetime was known as the woman with the world's smallest waist, was tight-laced throughout her marriage to a corset aficionado. At the height of her tight-lacing, she had a waist measurement of a hand span (13 inches). She was an obvious forerunner of the contemporary group of body artists known as the Modern Primitives, of whom Fakir Musafar is unacknowledged leader. Musafar, who took his name from an Indian Fakir who penetrated his body with daggers, experimented with his body from a very early age in the 1940s. He became excited by the tight waist-cinching belts worn

by the Ibitoe in Papua New Guinea. The belts formed part of a ritualistic rite of passage undergone by tribesmen on their entry to puberty. As Musafar explains:

> When a Papuan boy gets to an age at which an English boy begins
> to think about taking to stand-up collars ... he crushes his waist into
> a wooden belt so tight that his ribs protrude over it like the chest of a
> pouter pigeon. The belt terminates at the back in a kind of tail that trails
> upon the ground. The more wasp-like his waist becomes, the more airs
> the boy gives himself. When he has assumed this wooden belt he is called
> Ibitoe and becomes entitled to all privileges of a full-grown man ... [25]

Musafar subverted the Ibitoe ritual into a regime of body discipline for fetishistic effect and sexual play. He says of a tight-laced corset: "It enhances sexual experiences. There's nothing like being extremely tight-laced yourself as a male and making love with a woman who's extremely tight-laced. This is something you cannot experience any other way – all your internal organs and your sexual components are in different positions, with different tensions and so on – there's a mechanical basis for this. It's very ecstatic."[26]

By the 1980s and 1990s, the formerly taboo signifiers of fetishism had variously diffused into fashion through punk, Goth, the magazine *Skin 2*, and those whom anthropologist Ted Polhemus calls "Pervs." Members of an international subculture in Europe, Pervs, Polhemus explains, are committed to "exploring a new sexuality – one which seeks to replace the casual 'Your place or mine' promiscuity of the 1960s 'sexual revolution' with an approach that is more relationship-based, and more ritualistic."[27] Rubber and PVC corsets made by companies such as Stormy Leather, Waist and Stays, and Vampire Technology are associated with this scene. These corsets have had a direct impact on contemporary attitudes to dress in club culture.

In the 1990s the corset completely changed its meaning in popular culture. Once a symbol of women's oppression, it now stands as an icon of Girl Power, sported as outerwear by "Brit-Pop birds." Mr Pearl, once part of the fetish underground, is now orthodox, cinching Posh Spice Victoria Adams into her Vera Wang wedding dress; and Basia Zarzycka, based in Sloane Square, London, designs corsets as outerwear for her Knightsbridge clients.

OPPOSITE Janet Reger, dubbed the "Queen of Luxury Lingerie," uses the signifiers of corsetry such as boning and lacing to create a version that evokes a retro fantasy rather than functionality.

The fetish associations of the corset have now entered the vocabulary of mainstream fashion, appearing on the catwalks of Milan, London, Paris and New York. British designer Alexander McQueen's 1996 Dante Collection, for example, has given rise to a new generation of corset-wearing *femmes fatales*. Made of studded leather or engraved glass, McQueen's variations on the corset are not to be worn by the faint of heart. Women who do should be approached with caution, for the mute dominatrix of male fantasy may now have a voice.

Jean-Paul Gaultier is another designer who has used the corset, challenging orthodox ideas of gender on the catwalks of traditional Parisian haute couture. During his employment at Jean Patou he was horrified to see a model wearing heavy bandages to suppress her breasts so that the dress she was modeling would hang properly. This initial disgust led to a controversial series of negotiations around the construction of the corset, highlighting his interest in the exaggerated definition of the female form that it produced. In his hands, this intimate garment was recreated as outerwear. The Corset Dress of 1982 changed the breast from a soft, malleable object to a female weapon. For Madonna's Blonde Ambition tour in 1989, Gaultier dressed her in a man's pin-striped suit slit open at the breasts to reveal a corset. Cathy Schwictenberg, the cultural theorist, points out that "the corset worn over baggy suit pants undermines the traditional 'sexiness' of the corset itself."[28]

Both Thierry Mugler and Azzedine Alaia have used the techniques of the construction of the corset in their work, Mugler in his pneumatic fantasy women with their trademark hourglass silhouettes in black leather jackets in

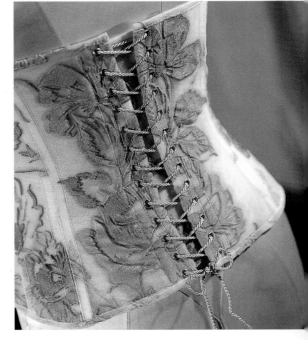

OPPOSITE & ABOVE Once underwear, the corset is now visible clothing. The aesthetic of the corset is incorporated in Basia Zarzycka's brocade bridal gown. She also uses decorative motifs derived from nature to make play with the "unnatural" corset.

1992–93, and Alaia – or the "King of Cling" as he was dubbed by the world's fashion press – in garments renowned for their display of the toned and muscled female body shape created by the newly fashionable gym culture of the 1980s. Alaia uses the stitching and seaming normally employed in corsetry to achieve the perfect fit of his clothes, combined with elasticated fabrics for maximum body exposure. His garments hold and control the body while still retaining their integral shape.

Christian Lacroix has used the template of the nineteenth-century cuirass bodice, itself an early example of the corset shape used as an upper garment, in his evening wear. Karl Lagerfeld and Gianni Versace have endlessly experimented with the corset to shape a woman's body into a fantasy ideal.

As Richard Martin has commented: "Even in an era when we know the cultural cast of a woman's body to be one of the last and most personal imprisonments of the doll's house, the dress object and body objectification still conspire, at least on occasion, to define body shape as sculpture. Indisputably, but often with argument that is hyperbole or specious, body shaping is related to cultural perspectives of the erogenous. Yet, the corset's revival in recent fashion may be as much about historicism and internal awareness in dress as it is about erogeny per se."[29] The corset, then, may not be a garment of subjugation but just another example of the post-modernist plundering of historical imagery in contemporary fashion to make play with traditional values of sexual subjection. As Martin astutely observes, "Irony and clever intelligence are the operative modes under which the corset has been reinstated."[30]

OPPOSITE & ABOVE The corset has undergone a complete change of meaning in popular culture and can no longer be regarded as signifying submission. As photographed by Karen Hatch, this corset-style top by Wit & Wisdom seems to suggest female armor rather than feminine acquiescence.

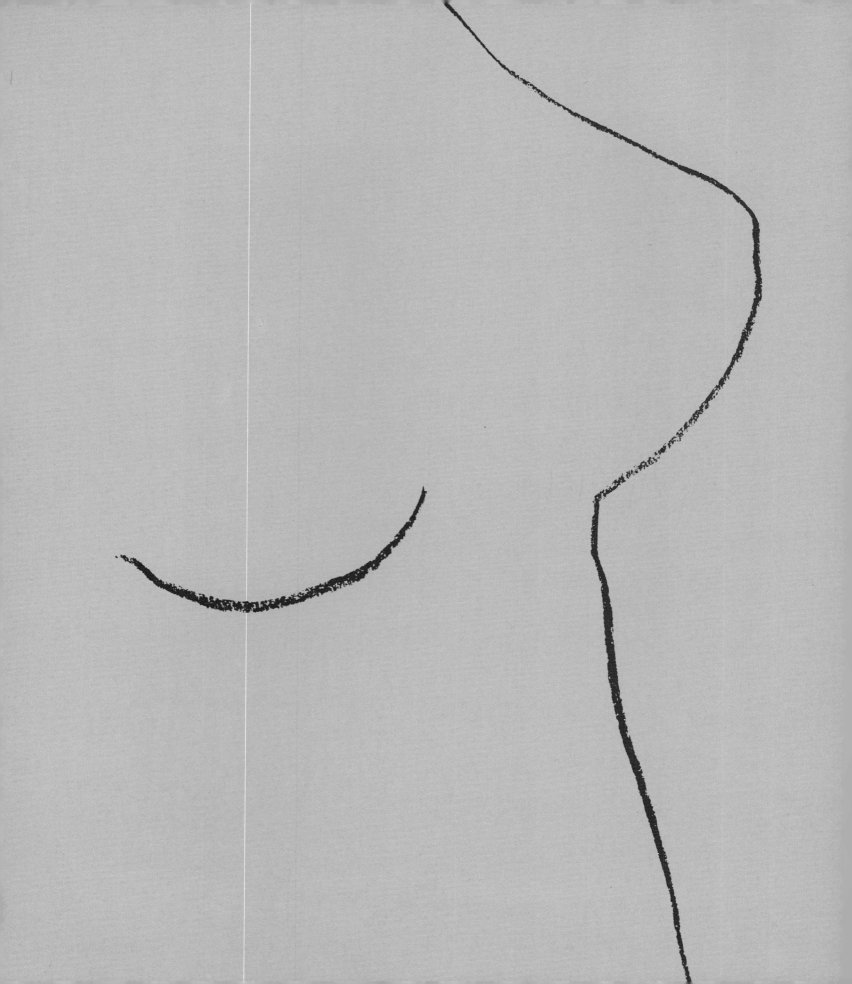

chapter two Cleavage Lines

cleavage lines

"You'd be surprised how tits figure in a girl's career." [1]

Louis B. Mayer, 1937

OPPOSITE The ubiquitous bra is one of the most obvious signifiers of femininity – here made even more so by the addition of bright pink frills. Illustration by Tanya Ling.

BELOW Frederick's of Hollywood have been renowned for their up-front bra designs since the 1950s. This lacy pink bra, entitled "Kiss," is said to create the ultimate cleavage.

The bra is a prime indicator of femaleness. Men in drag reach for the D cup to effect their transformation, while women who refuse to conform to the aesthetic dictates of a cross-your-heart number are regarded with disdain. Not much has changed since Roman times when many women wore scarves called *strophium*, not only to support their breasts but also to mark themselves out as civilized women. Bare-breastedness was taboo – the *strophium* was kept on even during love making. It was the barbarian woman who went about with her breasts unfettered – a precursor of the look espoused by radical feminists in the early 1970s. For them the bra was a symbol of the oppressive force wielded by men to keep women subordinate. Such feminists believed that women did not understand the physical nature of their oppression because they had been seduced by beauty rituals and pressurized to conform to society's ideals. By molding women's breasts, forcing them to conform to the dictates of a patriarchal, consumer-obsessed culture, the bra played a part in this process.

As the aesthetics of the breasts change, so do bra styles. Corsets had gathered breasts from underneath but the bra followed the principle of suspension from the shoulders to support the breasts from above. A fashionable New York debutante, Mary Phelps Jacob, who used the pseudonym Caresse Crosby, designed one of the first modern bras. In 1913, reacting to the restriction of the whalebone corset, she fashioned a rudimentary bra that contained and separated the breasts using two handkerchiefs, a length of ribbon and a little help from her maid. This was the first boneless bra to leave the midriff free. The patent was sold to the Warner Company, now one of the biggest bra makers.

Men have always been in awe of breasts, those most obvious signifiers of femininity. Cecil Saint-Laurent, an underwear historian, feverishly describes the early bra-type garments worn by the women of Crete in 2000 BC. These archaic designs, used primarily for display, exposed the breasts while aggressively thrusting them forward. Saint-Laurent sees these early breast supports as sexual above all, worn by aggressive dominatrices. He rather lasciviously describes the Cretan female as "lush-fleshed and whetted by her swollen underclothes, the make-up garish on her face, (she) evinces a violent desire to seduce, an awesome bitch."[2] The bitch with breasts, who inspired fear in the male onlooker, obsessed moralizers in Medieval Europe who condemned the overt display of that particular erogenous zone. Jan Hus, a writer of the time, raged against women "who wear gowns so deeply and so widely cut at the neckline that fully half the breast is exposed, so that their bursting flesh may be seen anywhere and by all, at the temple before the priests and clergy, at the market, and especially at home. The covered part of the breast is so emphasized, so artificially swelled and made prominent that it resembles two horns. These same horns are lifted very high and artificially projected forward, even when nature has not supplied women with such large endowments; at last, thanks to the shape of the bodice and an excess of clothing, the horns of the breasts rise upward."[3]

Despite Hus' alarm, women throughout the ages have continued to resort to fakery to achieve a little more of what God has given them. In the 1790s a "bosom friend" was the colloquialism used to describe a false breast made of wadding, which was inserted into garments to give a little extra "oomph" – a

OPPOSITE At the turn of the twentieth century breasts are the prime focus of the erotic gaze. Thus the goal of bra designers in creating models like the Wonderbra has been to perfect the combination of maximum uplift with the minimum of discomfort.

OPPOSITE Club culture has influenced bra design in the 1990s. This purple vinyl number from Sh!, more bikini top than bra, is for display as outerwear. The wet-look material gives a metallic sheen at odds with the soft malleability of the breasts beneath.

ABOVE This bra and briefs set by Bjorn Borg uses the aesthetics of minimalism to achieve a seductively streamlined effect. The traditional display of cleavage has been denied.

forerunner of the padded Wonderbra, the success story of the 1990s. Early examples of false breasts include eighteenth-century versions made of wax to be worn under light muslin dresses *à l'antique*. By 1885 it was possible to purchase a pair made of indestructible India rubber, and by the 1950s inflatable bras helped in the general deception. One bra historian writes of how "falsies" of this type could sometimes create a sensation, describing this formal occasion:

One lady was singled out above the others for the elegance of her figure and the perfection of her attire. In the quarter hour before dinner, she was surrounded by a swarm of admirers, one of whom was so bold as to offer her the flower from his buttonhole. The gift was accepted, and, as the gown worn by this ravishing lady laced up behind, the flower was attached to her breast with a pin. Hardly had the guests taken their places around the table when a peculiar sound was heard, like the sighing of the south wind. When the lady's admirer turned toward her in astonishment, he was horrified to observe that the charms that had so enticed him were visibly diminishing ... The rounded forms had vanished by the time the soup course was half over.[4]

In the 1950s cotton wool was another favored stuffing. This was the decade of the breast. As the critic Peter Lewis writes, "The bust, bosom or cleavage was for the Fifties the apotheosis of erogenous zones. The breasts were the apples of all eyes. Never in this century had so much respect been paid to mammary

development. The very concentration on female breasts seemed to swell them with pride to melon-like proportion – or disproportion, for they would flatten and disappear just as mysteriously ten years later. Whole careers were built on breasts."[5] One explanation was that immediately after a war "the hypertrophied female breast functions as a sort of nourishing and consoling pillow."[6]

These hypertrophied mammoth projectiles poked through tight sweaters, the most notorious outline being Jayne Russell's in the 1943 film *The Outlaw*, which was banned until 1950. The film star had complained that bras either squashed her famous breasts too tightly or didn't give her enough support, leaving her to "jiggle," so multi-millionaire Howard Hughes, who produced the film, brought the principles of aero-dynamics to the rescue of the perfect shape. He used his engineering skills, formerly utilized in aircraft development, to construct a cantilevered bra to support Russell's assets. The cultural construction of the big-bosomed dumb blonde stereotype was aided by the invention in 1953 of Triumph's cone-shaped, circular stitched bra, sported by stars such as Brigitte Bardot, Marilyn Monroe, and Jayne Mansfield, whose 42 DD shape was reputed to have been insured for one million dollars.

To further enhance the projectile effect of the Fifties breast, extra stiffening was inserted into the ends of the cup points. Another classic, the Hollywood Maxwell by Berlei was available in pink, white, or black nylon, cotton batiste, and net, and finished with whirlpool stitching to give perfectly rounded contours and just the right degree of separation. This evocative finish was used as a metaphor for a certain kind of Fifties glamor in the designs of Jean-Paul

OPPOSITE Advanced structural engineering techniques have been employed throughout the twentieth century to create the ultimate bra design. This bra is by Warners.

BELOW In consumer culture women strive to make their bodies conform to the fashionable ideal. Bra designers have to be responsive to these changes. Bra by Kenzo.

OPPOSITE Frederick's of Hollywood responded to the post-WWII breast obsession by designing sexy bras which help breasts defy the laws of nature. A masterpiece of engineering, this bra is a much cheaper alternative to cosmetic surgery.

Gaultier in the 1980s and early 1990s. When drawing on this source of imagery Gaultier was recalling the mature, big-bosomed women of his formative years rather than the fragile waifs of today. The designer's silhouettes invoke strength rather than fragility, with an added injection of kitsch for the ironic sensibilities of his post-modern audience.

The Fifties also saw the rise of that revered institution, Frederick's of Hollywood. Established in 1946 by ex-G.I. Frederick Mellinger, the lingerie company now reputedly sells 50 million mail order catalogs a year. Mellinger began by asking fellow soldiers to describe their fantasy underwear for the girl back home. His findings led to a range of sexy underwear, with bras the best-sellers. His philosophy was direct: "The company designs each undergarment, whether it is a baby-doll night gown or push-up bra, to make a woman more alluring to a man and more attractive to herself when she looks in the mirror."

Mellinger's array of glamorous black lingerie was launched at the same time as the Hollywood "lifestyle" was becoming popular. Women could be film stars in their fantasy lives and men could reap the benefits by buying into the "Hollywood Profile" collection of pointed circular stitched bras or the push-up version called "Rising Star." Evocative styles such as "Missiles" were launched, the name operating in the same sub-textual way as the most popular shoe of the 1950s, the stiletto. These were powerful looks that could kill! In Mellinger's "Cadillac" bra "you came in looking like a Chevy and left looking like a Cadillac." It was the perfect garment for this "mammo-oriented" era when the "sweater girl" was queen of cultural icons. New men's magazines, such as

Playboy, promoted the image of the sophisticated man about town with a well stacked girl on each arm and feted breasts that defied gravity. Mellinger's bra designs with their advanced structural engineering techniques made this possible.

Agent Provocateur parodied and subverted these post-war fantasy styles in the late 1990s. Operating from a tiny shop in Soho, London, the proprietors Joe Corre (the offspring of the anarchic pair Vivienne Westwood and Malcolm McClaren) and Serena Rees sell daring lingerie to women "who are in control of their lives." Corre's approach to underwear is simple: "Throw off puritan values, dress up, and indulge yourself in the desires of the body. Sex is one of the few simple pleasures in life and should be enjoyed to abandon."[7]

One of the industries to make the most out of the post-war breast obsession is cosmetic surgery. A disease dubbed "micromastia" (meaning "small breasts") was on the rise by the 1950s, although strangely enough it had not existed in the 1920s and 1930s when breast ideals were very different, and bandeaux not unlike the Roman *strophium* were used to suppress rather than increase the breasts' profile.

By 1956 *Cosmopolitan* magazine, in an article entitled "Monroes on the Increase," declared that: "Emphasis in our

society on the beautiful bust has become so extreme that there was little surprise in psychological circles when a teenage girl just recently committed suicide because she was flat-chested. How much misery this condition causes is not known."[8] This view was reiterated in a pioneering article by plastic surgeon Milton T Edgerton and psychiatrist A R McClary. They wrote, "Literally thousands of women, in this country alone, are seriously disturbed by feelings of inadequacy with regard to concepts of the body image. Partly as a result of exposure to advertising propaganda and questionable publicity, many physically normal women develop an almost paralyzing self-consciousness focused on the feeling that they do not have the correct size bosom ..."[9]

By the end of the 1950s, women in the early feminist movement were beginning to react against such insidious beauty ideals: Simone de Beauvoir, Betty Friedan, and later Germaine Greer. Her provocative tome *The Female Eunuch* advocated a rejection of the bra. She argued that "a full bosom is actually a millstone around a woman's neck: it endears her to the men who want to make their mammet of her, but she is never allowed to think that their popping eyes actually see her. Her breasts ... are not parts of a person but lures slung around her neck, to be kneaded and twisted like magic putty, or mumbled and mouthed like lolly ices. The only way that women can opt out of such gross handling is to refuse to wear undergarments which perpetuate the fantasy of pneumatic boobs, so that men must come to terms with the varieties of the real thing. The vegetable creep of women's liberation has freed some breasts from the domination of foam and wire."[10]

The response to Greer's emotive mode of expression together with events such as the Freedom Trash Can performance of 1968 led to the popular media stereotype of the bra-burning man-hater. The urban myth of bra-burning seems to have been constructed from the protests made by a group of American feminists called the New York Radical Women at Freedom Trash Can who, on railing against the stereotypical beauty standards of the Miss America contest, dumped the instruments of their oppression into a dustbin. Nothing was burned – in fact, the N.Y.R.W. was refused permission to stage the bonfire it wanted – but some male journalists made a connection between the feminist protest and the radicalism of draft-card burnings at anti-Vietnam war demonstrations, and reported the fire as though it had actually happened.

The bra-less stance of these women was running concurrently in fashion and was dubbed the "liberated look." Mary Quant, the British fashion designer, had found the standard fancy Fifties bra uncomfortable. She complained: "I know I am always seduced myself by the prettiest, frilliest, laciest bras that look so good when you're half undressed. But under a dress, they are nothing but unsightly lumps and bumps."[11] Rudi Gernreich, the avant-garde couturier, had designed the "no-bra bra" as early as 1964, which covered rather than molded the shape of the breasts.

OPPOSITE Feminists in the early 1970s rejected the bra as a symbol of women's oppression. By the 1980s and 1990s bra advertisers had co-opted the language of liberation to refigure the push-up bra as a symbol of girl power.

OVERLEAF The artist Chila Kumari Burman uses the Wonderbra as a metaphor for the dominance of Western images of femininity in global culture. Her photographic work "Hello Girls" combines white beauty ideals with traditional images of Indian women, commenting on beauty as a function of colonialism.

BELOW Although the 1990s was the decade of chasm cleavage, the small-breasted waif look was also lauded, particularly on the fashion catwalk: yet another example of the dichotomy inherent in the concept of the ideal female body.

One of the important breast legacies of feminist polemics was the gradual acceptance of the nipple in mainstream women's fashion. Bra manufacturers followed suit with styles like Dimanche's Dim, the first seamless bra and Gossard's Glossies, a "nude" line revived in the late 1990s made of a sheer material which allowed a glimpse of erect nipple while still providing support. For the first time a clear indicator of female sexual arousal could be displayed through thin clothing while wearing a bra.

Institutions such as Frederick's of Hollywood began to come under fire from feminist attack in the 1970s, and the flagship store in Hollywood was picketed. Mellinger prophetically hit back with the slogan "the law of gravity will win out." He was right. There has been an overall trend towards larger breasts in the Western world both in fashion imagery and reality, helped by improved diet and health care. The contraceptive pill, initially lauded as a tool of women's sexual liberation, has had the side effect of dramatically increasing the size of some women's breasts, as has the increasing acceptability of breast augmentation among women of all classes and incomes. By 1973, Miss America's measurements had changed drastically from 30-22-32 (in 1921) to 34-21-34. Big-breastedness had become such a beauty norm that by the 1980s the model agent Eileen Ford admitted that breast implants were rife among the models she promoted. This was despite the small-breasted look being promoted in fashion. The contradiction led to the designer Norma Kamali complaining, "When I'm thinking about

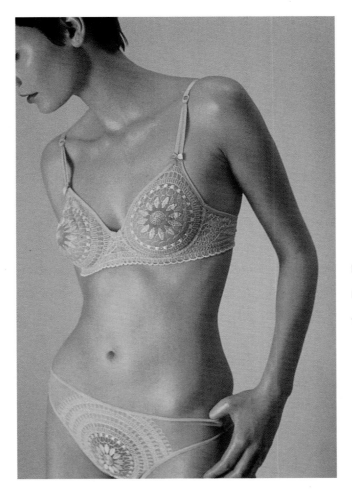

LEFT Nina Ricci's bra design makes oblique reference to the bra as female armor, the concentric circles delicately mirroring the look of a female warrior's breast-plate.

fashion, I think of perky little firm breasts that can go bra-less and not bounce or hang, and then I talk to men and realize that they like big tits."[12] There is an ambivalence here, though, for although many men fantasize about big breasts, as pornography sales testify, they also remind them of mother, which accounts for the distaste that arises when women breastfeed in public. Maternal breasts cannot also be sexual: that way psychological confusion lies.

Whatever the psychological issues, men's taste for a good pair of "hooters" won out by the late twentieth century as sales of Chantal Thomass, Janet Reger, and La Perla – the Rolls Royce of underwear design – testify. (There is even a chain of successful restaurants in America operating under this name complete with over-developed waitresses.) Although the waif look was pioneered by the supermodel Kate Moss on the high fashion catwalk, the 1990s was the decade of chasm cleavage. The Bra Wars of 1994 make this clear.

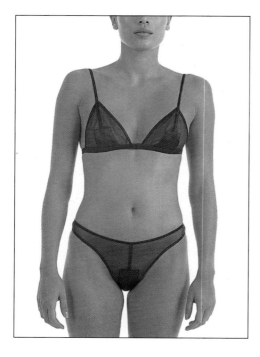

ABOVE The translucency of this design by Alessandro dell 'Acqua belies the fact that the nipples and pubic hair are made invisible beneath strategically placed markers.

Step into the ring Gossard Ultrabra and Playtex Wonderbra, slugging it out for market share. After the charms of the Wonderbra were extolled in British *Vogue* in 1992 and 22,000 were being sold every week in Britain, Gossard's license to produce the Wonderbra expired. Playtex snaffled it, and the bra was relaunched using the supermodel Eva Herzigova. The now infamous "Hello Boys" series of advertisements caused sales to soar, with Macy's reputedly selling 3,000 of the bras a day. Brian Duffy, who worked on the campaign, comments, "When the Wonderbra ad came out I think it turned people's thinking about underwear and underwear advertising upside-down. Here was this self-confident, provocative woman, using her sexuality. Women loved it, and before we knew where we were, we had a marketing phenomenon on our hands."[13] Gossard hit back with the Ultrabra and, in 1999, the Ultrabra Super Boost, which claimed to give the biggest cleavage ever "or your money back."

Fashion designers had also been commenting on the bra: Westwood's Buffalo Girl Collection of Autumn/Winter 1982-3 featured a large pink matronly bra worn as outerwear, and Gaultier used two fezzes, the tassels on the hats aping those used in a stripper's dance routine. Madonna showed off her bra straps in the 1985 film *Desperately Seeking Susan*, spawning a million imitators right into the late 1990s, and Thierry Mugler turned bra into car in 1990 with a bustier inspired by American auto styling. Many of these designs had fashion historian Colin McDowell decrying the fashion designer's view of the female figure in the 1990s. He believed that "many homosexual designers are repulsed by female breast as the outward and visible sign of the motherhood which

destroys the perfection of the female figure even as it menaces their own sexual world ... they hide their fear in laughter, by making fun of them and the femininity they signify. Conical bras, outrageously pointed and bearing no relationship to the shape of real breasts, are a cruel joke that brings women into the world of the crudest female impersonators, and puts them on the same level as the rugby player with coconuts under his jersey."[14]

However, if women do wear Gaultier's bra cones, for example, are they really the duped victims of a gay fashion designer's psychological turmoil? McDowell would have them thus, but post-feminists and presumably male designers would argue otherwise. Breasts in Gaultier's eyes do not need to be displayed purely for the delectation of men but show a new version of female power being played out "like a fantasy exaggerated,"[15] with the breast taking center stage as phallic symbol. And Valerie Steele sees another reason for the edginess some men feel about breast exposure. "Big breasts seem 'fancy' to some men, while small breasts seem 'plain' – a fairly obvious projection upward of anxiety about both penis size and female genitalia."[16]

Whatever the reasons, there is no getting away from the obsession with breasts and bras. Victoria's Secret, which specializes in glam undies and caters to the typical American woman who buys five bras per year, now sells 360 million copies of its catalog annually with a turnover of over $3 billion. A popular bar has opened in Manhattan's meat-packing district called "Hogs and Heifers." Female customers to this former strip club are invited to donate their bra, which is then hung from the rafters behind the bar for the delectation

OPPOSITE Triumph, one of the leading bra manufacturers, stays in step with the increasing bust size of women in the West. The company's DD to G range targets the bigger-breasted woman, usually denied seductive styles.

BELOW One of the classic poses of the underwear model – lying on the bed with hair tousled, arms back, and eyes half-closed, perhaps with some erotic fantasy in mind.

OPPOSITE The original Wonderbra by Playtex has iconic status. After the infamous "Hello Boys" advertising campaign featuring the supermodel Eva Herzigova, sales soared and a display of cleavage became the identifying badge of reconstructed feminists.

ABOVE This blue satin bra by Gossard can function with equal ease as either under or outerwear, as the lines of demarcation blur at the turn of the twentieth century.

of the customers. At the last count, the bras numbered 2,533, including those of actresses Drew Barrymore and Daryl Hannah, and actress Julia Robert's lacy black size 34 B Maidenform number.

So do women really receive any benefits from all this bra obsession and jostling in the bra market? The answer is a resounding "Yes." With competition so fierce bra manufacturers are continually having to improve their products and "market research shows that all women of all ages are looking for comfort," says Triumph spokesperson Sue Loder.[17] This has led to a dramatic change in the new directional styles of bras from push up 'n' plunge to the molded foam pod shapes for the cyber body of the twenty-first century pioneered by the French label Lejaby in 1995. As one journalist commented, "Were one ever to mentally undress Lieutenant Uhura from *Star Trek*, this is the underwear she would be wearing: smooth, futuristic, and unerringly pneumatic."[18] Nothing could be further from the seductive version of "femininity" promoted by the Wonderbra and its ilk. This is body armor for the cyber woman.

After a series of dramatic changes in construction and function, the bra is now the most complex garment in the underwear wardrobe, a masterpiece of engineering that can be composed of up to 43 separate parts. As Fontanel comments, "bras have now attained an unprecedented level of refinement and comfort."[19] Refinement may not be exactly the right terminology for the 1991 Mozart bra by Triumph, though. When the bra was fastened, a speaker secreted under the arm played "Twinkle Twinkle Little Star" and tiny lights flashed on and off. Still, there's a customer out there somewhere ...

LEFT Radical feminists viewed the bra as a symbol of women's oppression, repackaging the body for male consumption. Jean-Paul Gaultier reconfigures the bra as uniform for the female rebel-turned-seductress. The religious imagery reinforces the notion of woman as "temptation" – like Eve in the Garden of Eden.

LEFT Knickerbox takes a literal stance on the idea of the woman in control, portraying her as a flight controller who shows her frivolous side with maribou-trimmed lingerie.

OPPOSITE Wolford's starkly dramatic black underwear functions as smoothly as a machine. The woman as operator displays herself among obvious phallic references, the knobs and switches echoing the nipples hidden beneath her bra.

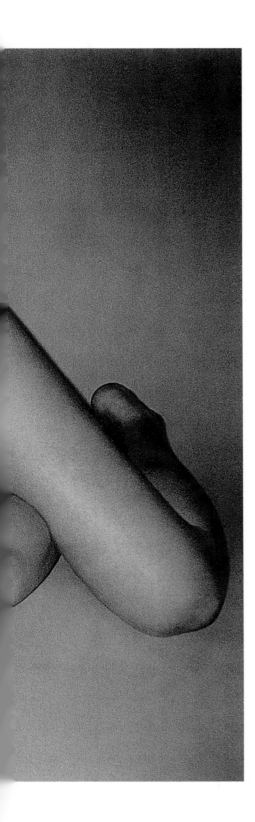

OPPOSITE Christy Turlington models a simple bra by
Calvin Klein, making minimalism sexually provocative.
"Less is more" is a perfect dictum for this underwear aesthetic.

RIGHT Alessandro dell' Acqua has a different take on
minimalism, designing "big" underwear which is perfectly suited
to the contemporary trend for transparent undergarments.

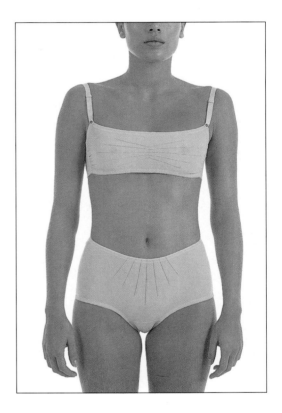

OPPOSITE & BELOW French fashion designer Nina Ricci uses traditionally feminine references placing women firmly within the realms of nature. One example is this floral, lace-trimmed ensemble in silk, with delicate shoe-string straps.

ABOVE The masquerade of femininity is laid bare: a careful construction of eyeliner, lipstick, pearls, and a black bra.

RIGHT The bustier is one of the most frequently appropriated lingerie styles for outerwear – offering more coverage than a bra, and more scope for shaping and decoration. This demure design from Sh! has a retro Edwardian feel.

ABOVE Competition in the bra market is fierce, which is to

the advantage of the female consumer. The plain white bra,

such as this one by Debenhams, London, now comes in a mind-

boggling array of styles, strap configurations, and fabrics.

OPPOSITE One of the most important breast legacies

of the feminist movement has been the acceptance of the

visible nipple in women's fashion.

OPPOSITE This dusky lilac bra shows how far removed bras have come from their original function. Designed by the cult London label Beau Bras, it cheekily presents the breasts as a birthday gift complete with ribbon tie.

BELOW Today the huge variety of bra styles mirrors the multiplicity of looks available to the woman of fashion, whether she opts for utilitarian function, overt sexiness, romance, or a combination of any of these.

chapter three Hip Zone

hip zone

"Underneath, cami-knickers with a French lace trim, lilac satin for me, crushed rose crêpe for her. Tasty, eh?"[1]

Angela Carter

That most prosaic of underwear designs, underpants are perhaps the most intimate garment of all. Their direct contact with the genitals makes them taboo yet the butt of jokes. And by hiding the ultimate prize, the vagina, their allure is intensified. From Marilyn Monroe's exposure in 1955 of surprisingly big knickers in *The Seven Year Itch* to the saucy seaside postcard on which an indiscreet flash leaves vulpine men panting, underpants come in many guises. Superman wears his on the outside and remains surprisingly cool, although when the ex-British Prime Minister John Major is drawn in the same get-up by the cartoonist Steve Bell he becomes a pathetic figure in his droopy drawers. In the 1920s schoolgirls wore embarrassingly large knickers made of denim so "thick and hot I thought I would be permanently scarred," which were "changed once a week,"[2] recalls underwear historian Rosemary Hawthorne.

By the 1990s it had became *de rigueur* to show off a big pair of pants under the transparent outerwear designs of Versace or Antonio Beradi, although these underpants were to be changed at least once a day. This deliberate anti-erotic look diffused the potential vulgarity of transparent fashions, making the wearers look chic rather than tarty as all was now safely gathered in.

According to the underwear historian Cecil Saint-Laurent, women first started wearing what we would now consider to be underpants during the Renaissance out of a sense of propriety. One writer of the time described their myriad uses: "In addition to helping [women] keep clean and protecting them from the cold, they prevent their thighs being seen if they fall off a horse.

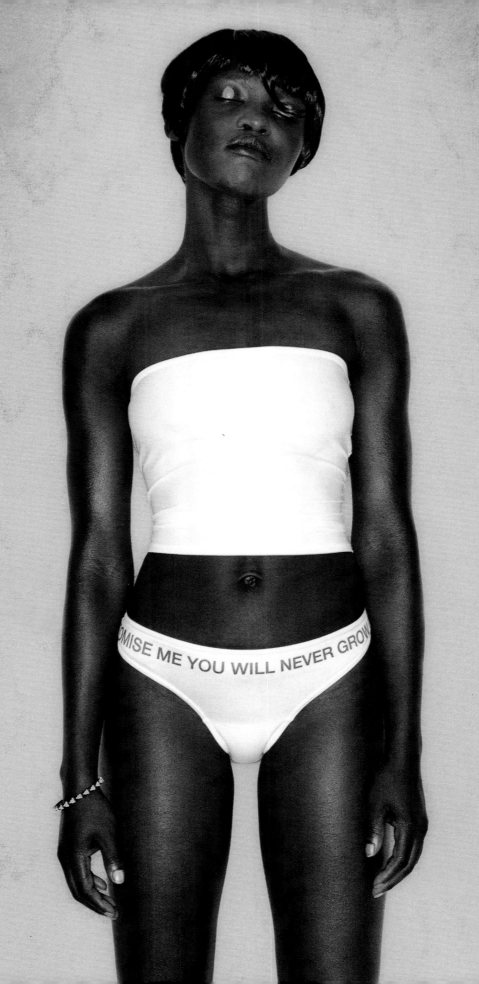

OPPOSITE Photographer Helmut Newton teams sheer black tights and towering stilettos in this sexually ambiguous image for Wolford. The undergarments make the body a fetish, standing for the private parts that remain hidden. The models refuse any contact outside of their own self absorption.

BELOW Functionality is absent in this pair of black rubber party pants by Sh! The frills are for exhibition rather than privacy, and can be buffed to a high sheen with a spray of silicone.

These drawers also protect them against adventurous young men, because if they slip their hands under their skirts they can't touch their skin at all."[3] Although they protected women's secret parts from prying hands, drawers also heightened sexual awareness and interest by drawing attention to those parts. Drawers were consequently considered exceptionally immodest. As a result, the first drawers-wearers were perceived as fast and loose, and the offending garments became an accepted part of the wardrobe of the courtesan. As the anthropologist Ted Polhemus comments, "For several hundred years drawers remained the uniform of prostitutes throughout Europe – which ensured that this intrinsically practical and modest garment could not be adopted by either the fashionable or by advocates of dress reform ... This was a problem which was exacerbated by the 'can-can', which specifically celebrated the erotic and disreputable connotations of this item of dress."[4]

The wearing of drawers was also considered unhealthy for women, who were urged to wear only petticoats under their skirts so that air could circulate freely around the genitals. However, a succession of severe winters in Europe in the 1840s, which wrought many a chill around the fundamentals, helped force a cultural change. By 1841 *The Handbook of the Toilet* was describing the fashion for drawers in France as "of incalculable advantage to women, preventing many of the disorders and indispositions to which British females are subject. The drawers may be of flannel, calico or cotton, and should reach

as far down the leg as possible without their being seen."[5] By the late nineteenth century the change was complete. As Saint-Laurent puts it, "A girl in drawers showed her virtue, one without her drawers her forwardness."[6] At this stage, drawers were designed so that each leg of the garment was separate and attached to the waist by tape. The crotchlessness of this underwear conveyed quite a different message to the fantasy versions now sold in sex boutiques, such as the successful British chain Ann Summers.

Sexuality and sensuality invaded women's underpants during the early twentieth century. The loose-fitting cami knickers of the 1920s were worn by Florenz Ziegfeld's chorus girls in his theatrically extravagant "Follies" for precisely that reason. Their loosely cut silk cami knickers were designed, according to Ziegfeld, to gently caress the inside of the girls' thighs so they would be in a state of heightened sexual awareness, which would in turn be projected to the audience. The sensuality of female underpants also drew the attention of male fetishists. Clarel Brand's book *Fetish*, published in 1970, describes the case of "Frederick C," who first became obsessed with women's briefs when he was fifteen. His mother was a dressmaker and one day she was fitting a client while Frederick was lying on the floor reading a book …

ABOVE In response to the demands of the skimpy fashions of the 1960s, Mary Quant designed liberating, functional, yet funky underwear for the young female consumer.

The dress had a flared skirt and the woman stood, quite unconsciously,
where I could see right up her skirt. She didn't have a slip on and for
the first time in my life I saw a woman's pants. I lay there, looking up
her long, beautiful legs. She had pink suspenders which disappeared

underneath her pants. They were white silk and I can clearly remember the way they hugged her bottom and showed off its shape: around the legs was a deep froth of frilly lace.[7]

Throughout the twentieth century women have had a mixed relationship with their underpants. From their original private state they have now become an intensely fashionable garment flashed by stars, such as Elizabeth Hurley and Julia Roberts, at premieres and fashion shows. Despite their flagrancy, in the late 1990s pants can also be the objects of derision and disparagement and the cause of stifled giggles, particularly if they fall down in public.

As a result of more than one hundred years of discretion and allusion about undies there is a glut of names by which to address what once was an offensive garment: knickers (derived from the original knickerbocker), britches, pantaloons, pantalets, drawers, panties, smalls, indescribables, bloomers, nether garments, step-ins, passion killers, kecks, grits and scanties. There is also the matching bra and brief set introduced in the 1960s, disposable paper panties invented in 1969, and the bikini brief of the 1970s. This particular piece of intimate apparel was designed to overcome the problem of the visible panty line (VPL), which appeared because of the tightness of women's jeans. The more adventurous woman wore a G-string. Originally used by strippers, this was composed of an elastic string that went around the waist and up between the buttocks, the underwear equivalent of dental floss. A more comfortable solution to the dreaded VPL was devised by the firm Sloggi – its briefs, made

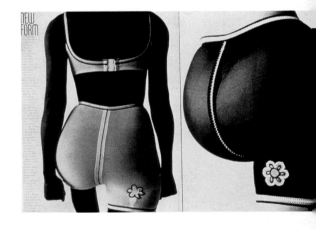

ABOVE Mary Quant's trademark daisy motif adorns the leg of these long-line drawers, the use of black and white edging making contemporary references to the fashionable Op Art movement of the 1960s, and painters such as Bridget Riley.

OPPOSITE Seen in silhouette, these stockings need careful handling at this stage of production, their flat forms to be filled out by the legs of women who had yearned for them in wartime.

95

RIGHT & OPPOSITE Minimalist fashion has made pantyhose an acceptable arena of decorative display. In these contemporary styles, Le Bourget uses motifs from the circus, a rich source of imagery that designers have often plundered.

of 95 percent cotton and 5 percent Lycra, clung closely and almost invisibly to the body.

In the late 1990s the thong became a garment of folkloric proportions due to Monica Lewinsky, who used hers to draw the attention of President Clinton. As the Starr Report puts it: "Ms Lewinsky and the President talked alone in the Chief of Staff's office. In the course of flirting with him, she raised her jacket in the back and showed him the straps of her thong underwear."[8] The President understood her particular use of the language of lingerie and responded like a bull to a red rag. The more conservative side of the underpants trade is maintained by institutions such as Marks & Spencer – according to the *Daily Telegraph* in 1988, "the guardians of the nation's nether regions." Their UK stores sell one and a half million pairs of knickers a week.

Hairiness is associated with masculine sexual power, smoothness with femininity. Stockings and pantyhose give the leg a smooth, hairless, and therefore feminine look. The first stockings were usually black or white but, with the advent of short skirts in the 1920s, "black stockings began to produce a somewhat startling effect. They pointed like two black sign posts to the lingerie above, and transformed what had been a mere suggestion to masculine interest into a positive invitation to set forth on a voyage of discovery," writes costume historian Lawrence Langner.[9] The introduction of flesh-colored stockings apparently stopped this sexual fervor. Garters were favored over garter belts, or suspenders, but had virtually disappeared by the late 1900s.

The invention of nylon in the late 1930s by the Dupont company gave stockings a closer, "nuder" fit, causing Lawrence Langner to call nylon "the invention of the devil himself. For who but the devil would think of transforming the coal with which he feeds the everlasting fires of hell into the filament used in the nylon stockings which lure so many sinners into his clutches."[10] The wearing of mini skirts in the 1960s helped accelerate the demise of stockings, and in 1965 Chelsea girls prized pairs of pantyhose by Mary Quant with their trademark daisy motif. Garter belts were re-introduced as erotic wear for the bedroom by the 1970s. Inspired by the psycho-dramas rehearsed in Helmut Newton's fashion photography, garter belts, and seamed stockings appeared in a darkly sensual undie underworld of gigolos, androgynes, and mannequin women.

This essentially male-pleasing vision was subverted by punk women who wore torn fishnet stockings with Dr Marten boots and rubber mini skirts short enough to reveal a flash of stocking top. In this arena, traditionally "sexy" underwear was paraded as a mark of feminine defiance, and the garter belt became a marker of the sexually confident woman on top rather than the saucy pin-up of the past. From 1982 to 1985 garter belt sales rose by 150 percent in

OPPOSITE Fogal's surrealist image places a model in a traditional glamor pose wearing red-for-danger lingerie within the heat of a vast, empty desert. Whose attention does she hope to attract?

ABOVE The controlling properties of Lycra have seen a renaissance in body-shaping underwear in the late twentieth century. This design by Charnos invites comparison with the 1950s girdle.

Britain as women strove for power in the boardroom and bedroom. Hold-ups provided a gusset-free alternative without the paraphernalia of buttons and clips. Opaques deflected the gaze held by the previously nude styles.

Pantyhose no longer pretend to be natural. New Age road protesters wear bold striped pairs, and thick woolly ones can be worn with shorts in winter. The recent vogue for kitten heels and pencil skirts has encouraged the revival of sheer looks for legs, while the retro-kitsch 1960s movement inspired by parodies such as the Austin Powers films has led to a fad for white, patterned and space age styles. As the psychologist Flugel presciently observed in 1930:

> *Recently, there has taken place a revolutionary change in our ideas concerning the respectability of the feminine leg, and women now show freely what has, with very few exceptions, been draped since the dawn of Western civilizations. How great is the change that has taken place in a relatively few years can best be realized when we remember that, not so long ago, it was indelicate not merely to show the leg but even to refer to it – at least by its proper English name.*[11]

There is now no hard-and-fast rule about how little or how much leg is shown. Liz Hurley, for instance, can wear a skirt slit high enough to reveal a flash of sequined knickers at a society wedding. The exposure of the leg, once one of the greatest social taboos, is accepted at the most formal of functions, especially if encased in a stocking's second skin.

OPPOSITE Girly NYC uses 1970s styling to meet the current fashion obsession with retro. The consumer takes refuge in a past already run, in defense against the unknown of a new millennium.

BELOW Echoing the look of frilly tennis pants, the combination of red, associated with erotic underwear, and virginal white lace creates a garment of contradiction for Sh!.

OPPOSITE The creation of hold-up stockings combined the function of pantyhose with the eroticism of the visible thigh, an obvious referent of the increasingly anachronistic garter belt, now a garment of ritualized display.

LEFT Le Bourget's pantyhose design here transforms the naked leg into a stick of striped candy – creating both a visual and oral pathway to the intimacies above.

OPPOSITE Like the feather tails of the peacock, much of women's underwear is designed for "performance." Here, Nina Ricci's knickers are little more than a froth of white lace, which makes them seem intended for pure erotic display.

RIGHT The underwear styles of the working girl have been subverted by women who now feel confident in expressing their own active desires. Balcony bra, pants, and garter belt from Sh!.

RIGHT The woman who buys into this underpants design by Miu Miu is crossing the line between underwear and outerwear. The garment could be worn on its own as clubwear or under contemporary transparent fashions.

OPPOSITE Designer Liza Bruce blurs the lines between swimwear and underwear with this design which breaks the rules of traditional fashion vocabulary. This is underwear as outerwear, to be teamed with cardigan and summer tan. Photograph by Steve Hiett.

ABOVE Decorative underwear can be functional, too, these days due to advances in new materials and construction techniques. These high-cut panties by Playtex mirror changes which first appeared in women's swimwear in the late 1970s.

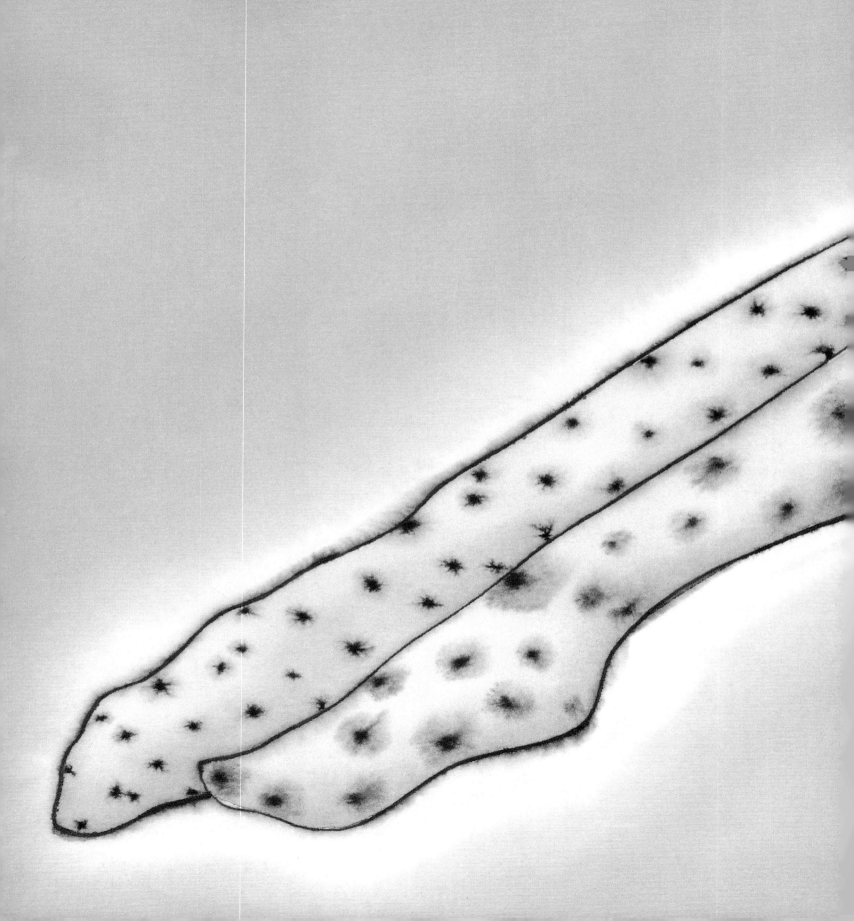

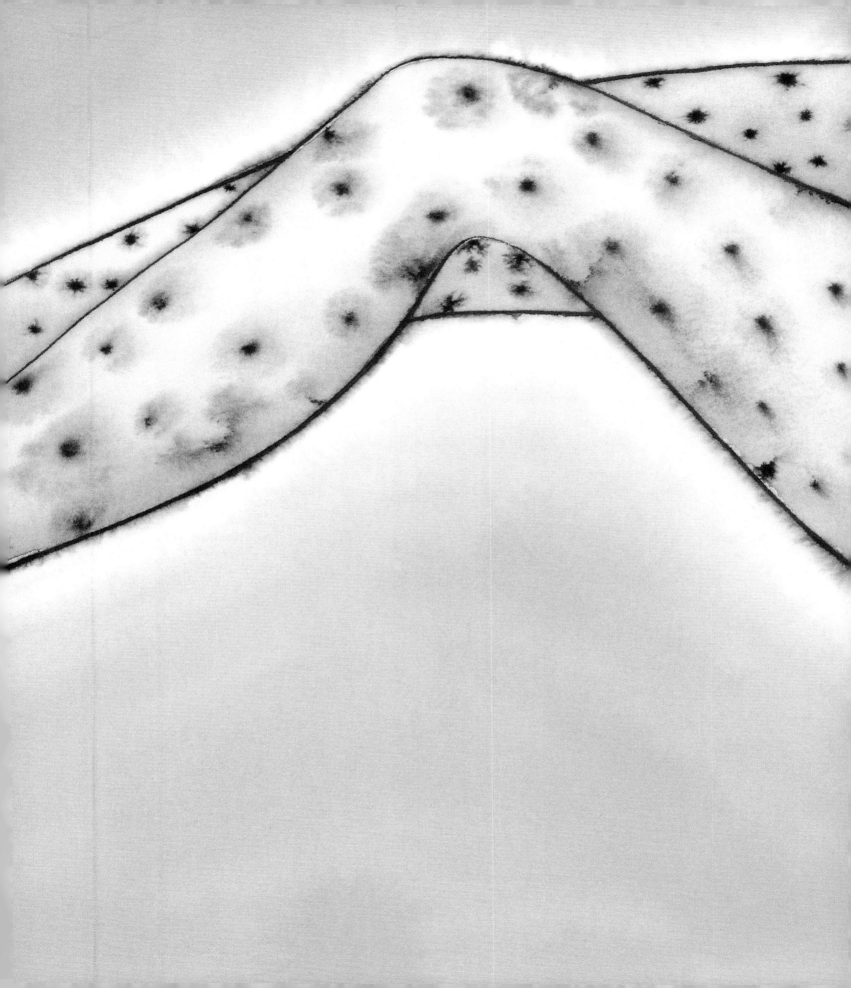

PREVIOUS PAGE Stockings and pantyhose act aesthetically to give the female leg a smooth, hairless appearance. The invention of nylon gave stockings a closer fit as the exposure of the leg became more and more acceptable. Illustration by Kareem Iliya.

RIGHT & BELOW The power of the imagery used in these Janet Reger advertisements comes from blatant references to the wearing of underwear as a prelude to sexual activity. With not a hint of functionality, these expensive wisps of lace that stand for panties are discarded in the sterile confines of a hotel room at the start of an anonymous sexual encounter.

BELOW Knickerbox's rich floral design seems at odds with the sterility of the airplane's interior, in this photograph by Willy Camden. The model's lack of concern at the public exposure of such intimate apparel reflects a confidence in her underwear.

RIGHT Helmut Newton subverts the aesthetics of underwear advertising in his campaign images for Wolford. The models have no interest in the spectator or consumer – they are immersed in their own erotic encounter.

RIGHT This design by Joop manages to combine delicate, lacy looks with athletic fit, the G-string back enhancing the garment's function as a tool for sexual display.

OPPOSITE Much recent underwear design has been in dramatic reaction to the minimalism of women's fashion in the 1990s. The simplicity of, say, Prada outerwear is in stark contrast to these bits of rococo frippery worn beneath. Barely-there panties by Beau Bras are held on with ribbons.

OPPOSITE A woman can use lingerie to invoke her favorite fantasy. This advertisement by Aristoc plays on associations with one of the most popular fantasies – the woman as up-market strip artist who confidently sashays onto the stage in the ubiquitous black stilettos and shiny black underwear.

RIGHT In contrast with the image opposite, Fogal shows the moment of disrobing as one fraught with anxiety. Although the elements that make up the underwear combination are almost identical, the carefully placed footwear and sideways glance give an air of intimacy and convey a fear of exposure, as compared with the confident narcissism of the stripper.

LEFT The performance artist Vanessa Beecroft poses her models
awkwardly and seemingly without artifice to convey a sense of
the backstage of a beauty contest or fashion show. This realism
is heightened by the wearing of pantyhose over visible underwear,
which deconstructs the usually highly finished glossiness of
contemporary images of women in consumer culture.

LEFT A less retro but equally evocative image for Aristoc using the same powerful signifiers of dangerous female sexuality – high heels and black stockings.

OPPOSITE Shades of the showgirl in this photograph by Fred Corcoran. The combination of girdle, stockings, and fluffy mules evokes a period nostalgia and brings to mind iconic figures such as Marlene Dietrich in *The Blue Angel*, a woman who uses her destructive powers to the detriment of men.

chapter four Boudoir Chic

boudoir chic

"Brevity is the soul of lingerie."[1]

Dorothy Parker

OPPOSITE The vocabulary of underwear developed and extended into decorative lingerie in the early twentieth century. The increase in the popularity and thus use of lingerie mirrored women's gradual freedom from the constraints of Victorian morality and notions of appropriate femininity to become both more sexually and socially independent. The language of lingerie has now been fully incorporated into fashion, as in this dress by Blumarine.

When the American designer Bob Mackie presented his premiere collection of "fantasy lingerie" in the 1980s, it is significant that he did so by making direct reference to the origins of lingerie in the late nineteenth and early twentieth centuries. In her book *Backlash,* Susan Faludi described the scene thus: "Six models in satin panties and lace teddies drifted dreamily into view and took turns swooning on the main stage prop – a Victorian couch. The enervated ladies – 'Sopha,' 'Désirée,' 'Amapola' – languorously stroked their tresses with antique silver hairbrushes, stopping occasionally to lift limp hands to their brows, as if even this bit of grooming overtaxed their delicate constitutions."[2]

This invocation of a mythical mix of Victorian and Edwardian eras has become a cliché of lingerie advertising and connects our late twentieth-century sensibilities with the pioneers of lingerie design – women such as the English designer Lucile. This forthright aristocrat, who was only prepared to use girls weighing over ten stone as models and was one of the survivors of the *Titanic* disaster, introduced a staid public to delicately fashioned camisoles, peignoirs, and petticoats of lace, chiffon, and crêpe de Chine. Once considered the province of the prostitute, these garments were being worn to put the fun back into male–female relationships, although any color other than white was still considered rather rude.

By the Edwardian era, expressions of a healthy heterosexuality within the confines of matrimony were becoming acceptable as a generation attempted to differentiate itself from the supposedly staid Victorians. A hard line was still taken with "promiscuity" – that is, sex among the single – but many "New

OPPOSITE Lingerie plays on the usual associations of women with frills, bows, and lace, but the delicacy inherent in undergarments such as these by Divertimenti now speaks of a sexually assertive rather than passive woman.

Women," suffragette-inspired females who were demanding more equality in the class-obsessed culture of Edwardian society, were no longer prepared to "lie back and think of England."

Lingerie provided one escape from the traditional nineteenth-century notions of morality and respectable womanhood, as fashion historian Jennifer Craik has observed. She writes: "Sexual overtones were deliberately attached to the contradictions between the outer and the inner messages of femininity. In order to distinguish female and male underwear, the female garments were made as 'feminine' as possible by excessive attention to special 'cuts,' 'soft' fabrics, and decoration."[3] It was in this century that the French writer Octave Uzanne compared a woman in lingerie to "a tinted flower, whose innumerable petals become more and more beautiful and delicate as you reach the sweet depths of the innermost petals. She is like a rare orchid, who surrenders the fragrance of her mysteries only in the intimacies of love."[4] At the time of his writing an argument raged about women's underwear. There were two camps: the sober rational look inspired by the redoubtable Dr Jaeger, who advocated the use of wool next to the skin for reasons of hygiene and health, and the much more erotic, sensual form of underwear known as lingerie.

The more liberal ladies' magazines of the Edwardian era saw sensual underwear as the perfect garb for the woman who wanted to please her husband within the sanctity of marriage. One even wrote that "the transparent nightgown is for the woman what the robe is to the lawyer." Valerie Steele, on surveying early twentieth-century attitudes to lingerie, comments: "More women

ABOVE The contemporary fashion for underwear as outerwear can cause confusion. The distinction between the two is unclear in this girlish combination by DKNY.

OPPOSITE The agonies a fashionable woman is supposed to undergo to achieve the culturally appropriate look are parodied in this contemporary illustration by Richard Gray. The mannequin's fantasy corset is tight laced.

BELOW Lingerie does not need to look overtly sexualized to be counted as such, as this vest and pantie ensemble by Kenzo shows, with its deep red color and hint at sheerness.

were dressing attractively for intimate moments and for their own pleasure."[5] "Lovely lingerie" did not belong "only to the fast," wrote a female fashion journalist in 1902, adding that "dainty undergarments are not necessarily a sign of depravity. The most virtuous of us are now allowed to possess pretty undergarments, without being looked upon as suspicious characters."[6]

With the increasing use of the Singer sewing machine within the home in the twentieth century, handmade lingerie assumed even more of a social significance, becoming a marker of high status affordable only by the very few. Peignoirs, camisoles and teddies became "non-garments characteristic of what you might call hyper-culture," as the novelist Angela Carter puts it, adding:

> *Others are some furs, evening dresses and ball gowns, real jewelry. All are, first and foremost, items of pure conspicuous consumption. Yet they also fulfill elaborate ritual functions. They are the garb for the pursuit of anti-nature. This includes the opera, eating in restaurants, parties, and, increasingly, sexual relations in which the gibbering old id, the Beast in Man, the manifestation of nature at is most intransigent, is scrupulously exiled. In hyper-culture human relations are an art form.*[7]

The first items of seductive lingerie were worn by the New Women of the 1890s under relatively austere garments such as the "tailor-made," an off-the-peg suit. The New Woman was presented by the conservative press as a symptom of cultural anxiety, embodying a blurring of gender at the *fin de siècle*,

a decadence also expressed in the lifestyles of artists and writers such as Aubrey Beardsley and Oscar Wilde. To offset the "mannish" accusations directed at the New Woman, a more traditional femininity was being reinforced by the aficionados of lingerie composed of silk, satin and chiffon. In a pertinent segue, sales of exotic lingerie went up exponentially in the 1980s with the rise of women in the executive arena who favored lacy camisoles under power suits.

The camisole was originally derived from a decorative waist-length garment with an embroidered and pleated front and shoulder straps, which was worn over the corset in the nineteenth century for warmth and modesty. In the 1990s a similar turnaround occurred with the slip, an undergarment popular in the 1950s, now converted by designers such as John Galliano into a simple, slinky dress with trim to be worn as outerwear.

New items of lingerie have continued to be invented. The development of artificial fiber has been crucial to the development of lingerie as it is much lighter than the usual cotton or linen. Rayon, for instance, democratized lingerie in the 1920s by being a relatively cheap fabric and thus making lovely undies affordable for many women. It was deliberately associated with notions of luxury by being widely known as "artificial silk." Petticoats were useless for the newly body-hugging flapper fashions of the 1920s, so the teddy was invented, named after its inventor, Theodore Baer. A combined chemise with short slip or panties, it was eventually worn as a piece of clothing in its own right in the 1970s, as designed by Janet Reger, the "Queen of Luxury Lingerie." Reger's lingerie, showing a "sophisticated carnality,"[8] decorated rather than dressed the

OPPOSITE By 1923 erotic lingerie was no longer just the working wardrobe of the prostitute, and the development of artificial fibers made lovely underwear accessible to many women. As the twentieth century progressed, new items of lingerie continued to be invented, and pale pink was coded as "feminine" when it came to underwear design, as evident in the Harrods catalog.

bodies of 1970s sirens Bianca Jagger and Angie Bowie, and is still a potent force in the market. The company La Perla, founded by Ada Masotti in 1954, also epitomizes the luxury of hand-crafted lingerie with its teddies, slips, and peignoirs.

Chantal Thomass is another name closely linked with top-of-the-range lace fripperies. Her collections, the first of which appeared in 1975, reflect the themes inherent in her ready-to-wear collections. Her clients include the singer and actress Cher and the French actress Catherine Deneuve. Thomass believes that "lingerie is something that you wear close to your skin and it is the first thing that a woman thinks of as she gets dressed in the morning, so her choice of lingerie will determine and affect her mood for the rest of the day. Her choice of lingerie will determine the way she walks, sits and moves all day long. I design lingerie to make women feel good; which is simple and comfortable."[9]

Lingerie is now more erotic than the nude body, the fabrics mirroring the feel of idealized flesh. It whispers of private

pleasures. To disrobe when clothed in exotic, functionless smalls is the equivalent of the Dance of the Seven Veils, and the use of lingerie in itself designates occasions as sexual.

Today lingerie and its relationship with sexual play are totally normalized and the two are entirely interrelated – one dresses rather than undresses for sex, "enriching your life through a non-garment."[10] Angela Carter, in her brilliant deconstruction of a Janet Reger catalog in 1977, argues that sexy lingerie "is part of the 'fantasy courtesan' syndrome of the sexy exec, a syndrome reflected admirably in the pages of *Cosmopolitan* magazine. Working women regain the femininity they have lost behind the office desk by parading about like a *grande horizontale* from early Colette in the privacy of their flats, even if there is nobody there to see."[11]

Men are also targeted in a variety of ways as consumers of lingerie. The Californian company Victoria's Secret had as its premise a lingerie boutique that men would feel comfortable going into, but the marketers also didn't want women to think a man was running it. Thus its sepia catalogs include a personalized missive from "Victoria" who is supposed to be in control. The story goes that if any customer asks to meet her she is 'traveling in Europe' while her company is busily selling an estimated six hundred items of lingerie per minute. Lingerie mail-order firms also sell to men themselves by having a range of large sizes that are by implication for men to wear. More recently there has also been the development of specialist catalogs, such as the Cascade group, which cater

ABOVE Girly NYC subverts the tackiness of cheesecake pin-ups and see through baby doll nighties to the delight of contemporary female ironists. Illustration by Susan San Giovanni.

OPPOSITE The corset dress, a staple of 1980s fashion popularized by stars such as Madonna, has appeared in the collections of many of the major high fashion designers.

OPPOSITE The teddy has become a standard of the lingerie repertoire since its invention by Theodore Baer in the 1920s. This 1990s equivalent by Janet Reger uses a combination of the 1980s "body" and the underwired bra to create a hybrid.

ABOVE The jokey phallic symbolism in this advertisement for Knickerbox underwear is further enhanced by that 1970s classic, the shag-pile carpet. It carries shades of *Wallpaper*-style irony.

to a gay male market, offering a nice line in lace panties as well as more curious items such as the "Gladiator" or "Sling Shot Suspender Thong" available in "fuchsia, coral, or wet black."[12]

By the 1990s lingerie could be simple or frilly. The designer Donna Karan has two collections: her name underwear is understated – nude, sheer and seamless – but the DKNY range is frippery, a candy-colored collection launched in 1999 using satin, ribbon, lace, and bows. The simple Egyptian cotton camisole worn by actress Nicole Kidman in Stanley Kubrick's last film, *Eyes Wide Shut*, has been a recent major lingerie seller. Made by the Hanro company, it is worn by Kidman "in a sex confession scene with her real-life and screen husband Tom Cruise, which 'might have charged the camisole with more emotion in the minds of our customers,' the Swiss firm's spokeswoman explains."[13]

The emotional charge of lingerie is a moot point. Its associations with sexual intimacy can create uneasy associations in the mind of the wearer. One journalist describes a friend who "reports how a gentleman once said to her, in a first moment of disrobing that had revealed a workday if gorgeous black bra: 'Were you thinking of me when you put that on?' She didn't know what to say. 'No, the idea of disrobing in front of you hadn't crossed my mind'? Or: 'Yes, I've been dreaming of this moment.' She found herself eyeing the bra with suspicion on subsequent occasions. Who was she putting it on for? Was it a pulling kind of a bra? Was it innately sexy? It always reminded her of him and later, when she fell in love with someone else, she had to put it away altogether because it brought the first man into the bedroom whenever she wore it."[14]

OPPOSITE Lingerie has now moved out of the bedroom, and garments such as this slip dress by Bella Freud are worn openly as outerwear. Teamed with kitten heels this look reflects the polymorphous perversity of femininity in the new millennium.

Lingerie has now moved out of the bedroom; even the slightly smutty baby doll nightie with matching puff panties, originally seen in the 1956 film *Baby Doll* starring Carroll Baker, has been reconstructed by Agent Provocateur and crossed over into fashion and club life. Slips, as formerly worn by Hollywood luminaries such as Elizabeth Taylor in *Butterfield 8* or Janet Leigh in *Psycho* in 1960, are now worn as outerwear designed by John Galliano. Designers such as Thierry Mugler, Giorgio Armani, and Ralph Lauren have changed lingerie into outerwear by using sheer chiffon, bustier tops, and slip dresses to conjure up the boudoir. In 1998 the Australian designer Colette Dinnegan's models took to the catwalk "in lingerie styles sweet enough to eat with a spoon,"[15] incorporating sheer drawstring teddies, knee-tie bloomers, and petticoat dresses in bourbon pink, peach, and cream.

So what is behind this resurgence in nostalgic lingerie? A sense of security in times past? The future is an unknown place that seems threatening, but the past has already run, so why not run it again? Perhaps, but the lingerie revival could also be read as a backlash against minimalism. To wear frippery such as lingerie is one of the most oppositional and unorthodox stances a woman can take in an era dominated by concerns of form following function.

ABOVE Caught unawares in their slips, or wearing fashionable summer dresses? The slip dress appears sexy precisely because it carries reminders of its original, intimate purpose.

RIGHT The softness and delicacy of the pale pink slip dress
is subverted by the strong, confident, almost predatory wearer
in this provocative illustration by Tanya Ling.

BELOW French Connection use the style of classic thermal
underwear to create a fresh, soft, comfortable combination of
matching vest and underpants.

LEFT Deadly serious in see-through black lace and fluffy mules, this model displays a look dubbed by the novelist Angela Carter as "the fantasy courtesan syndrome" – worn by working women to regain the femininity lost behind the office desk.

BELOW In contrast, the lighter, more ironic pose of the woman so confident in her sexuality she is prepared to be kitsch, in a snow white Cross Your Heart camisole set by Girly NYC.

ABOVE & BELOW This two-piece set by Warehouse epitomizes the appeal of delicate underwear bought by women to please themselves, not for the delectation of men.

RIGHT A black lace bra that could be underwear or outerwear, its relationship with sexual play completely normalized and thus acceptable in contemporary culture, where outward expressions of active sexuality are no longer taboo.

OPPOSITE Some garments are suffused with their own emotional associations, so much so that if a special relationship ends, items of intimate apparel have to be destroyed. Photograph by Karen Hatch, dress by Wit & Wisdom.

BELOW This dress by Karen Millen uses the processes of lingerie – in this case the corset – to invest it with erotic significance inspired by the hourglass shape of the 1950s starlet. Reinforcing the image are bright red lips and painted nails.

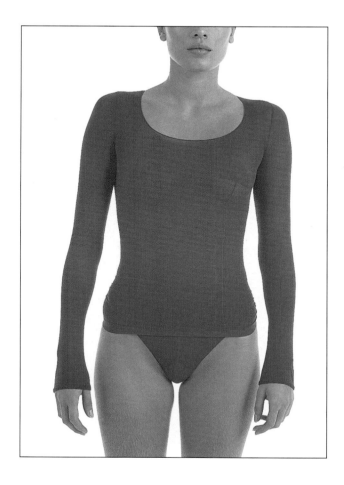

ABOVE This streamlined body suit by Alessandro dell' Acqua fits

like a second skin, ironing out imperfections – and at the same

time any blatant references to sexuality.

LEFT Sexual play seems to be the prime function of this transpar-

ent slip by Debenhams. Its very fragility, and the environment of

the bedroom, position it very clearly for display only.

OPPOSITE The detailed decoration of an item of lingerie flaunts its high status. A perfect example of conspicuous consumption, this colorful embroidered slip is designed by Joop. Only a few would be prepared to confine it to the boudoir.

BELOW A corset-inspired top and matching skirt from Sh! which evoke the image of the showgirl in a western saloon. Too glamorous in its own right to be hidden away, the ensemble is pure outerwear, designed particularly for club-goers.

RIGHT The slip dress, derived from a functional undergarment, has become a staple of the fashionable woman's wardrobe. It takes its inspiration from varied sources – from the silky, skin-hugging 1950s slip to the romantic Victorian petticoat.

OPPOSITE The delicate fabric of this little underwear/outerwear number by Blumarine is ignored in this advertising image, suggesting that those who can afford to buy it can afford to ruin it, too, during the morning after the evening before.

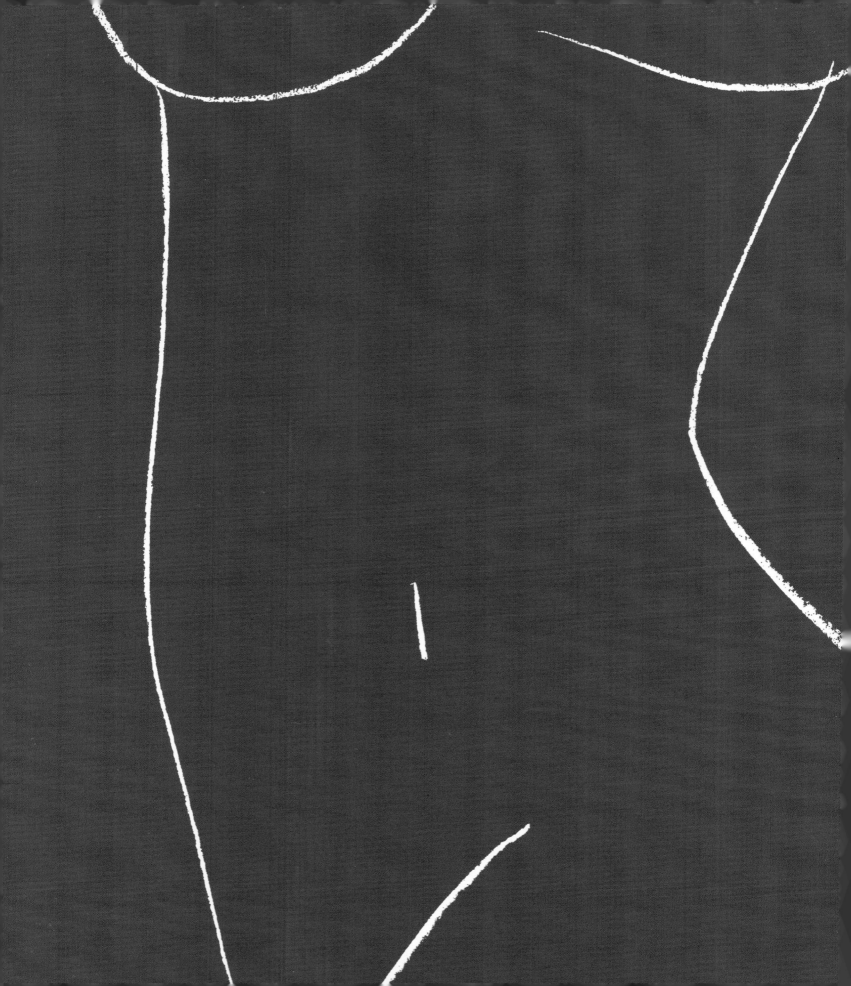

chapter five Athletic Ambition

athletic ambition

"He put the balls back into men's underwear."

Anonymous on Calvin Klein

ABOVE Damart, a company renowned for the thermal properties of its practical underwear, has re-branded itself in the 1990s as the fashion for function continues.

OPPOSITE This utility vest and pants combination has been given a dramatic twist by Knickerbox with the unexpected use of glossy crimson red. Photograph by Willy Camden.

According to writers Leonore Davidoff and Catherine Hall, the constructs of masculinity and femininity are "specific to historical time and place. They are categories continually being forged, contested, reworked and reaffirmed in social institutions and practices as well as a range of ideologies. Among these conflicting definitions there is always space for negotiation and change …"[1] Even that most gender-specific of fashions – underwear – has provided a means of expression for reassessing the notions of masculinity and femininity at the end of the twentieth century. It all began in 1993 with one of the most infamous ad campaigns of all time. Fashion photographer Herb Ritts had created a series of images for Calvin Klein underwear using the pop star Marky Mark (Mark Wahlberg), who had been the butt of a whispering campaign in music circles over the fabled size of his appendage, which the advertisements seemed to verify. When the Klein campaign was launched it caused a sensation: "Crazed fans broke the glass in dozens of New York bus-stop shelters to steal the poster: Klein installed a huge reproduction on a Times Square billboard so that he could view it from his car traveling to work."[2]

Klein's vision of underwear made a decisive break from the image of the cowboy in his red flannel combinations with buttons over the bum: now he was a god in a Lycra bodysuit, toned to perfection. It was a vision drawing on a trend that had begun in the 1980s – for the social and physical power of men to be expressed through the nude or semi-nude body rather than the pin-striped executive. By the late 1990s it was the norm for fashion designers like Giorgio Armani and Paul Smith to have their own ranges of male underwear and for

158

OPPOSITE The "body," a garment derived from the dancer's leotard and the 1970s body-stocking, has taken underwear into an entirely new and successful direction since its fashionable conception in the 1980s, by reducing it all to one simple garment.

the accompanying ad campaigns to invariably feature impossibly perfect male bodies sporting the designer wares. Men were now under the same pressures as women to conform to the prevailing advertising ideals – an anxiety expressed in the following UK newspaper article of 1999:

BELOW Georges Rech adds glamor to a simple camisole top, creating outerwear from a garment first designed to be worn over the corset in the nineteenth century for warmth and modesty.

> *Tim glanced at the billowing white cotton. They were the sort of form-hugging trunks usually advertised by young blades whose elaborately segmented stomachs bulge in a manner that suggests they are midway through digesting a radiator. Tim, who is at the point in his life when the nearest he gets to muscle definition is knowing where the hamstring is, was naturally shocked, not least by the manufacturer's name boldly printed across the waistband of the offending duds. He shooed them away with an indignant flick of his hand and words to the effect that his wife had clearly taken leave of her senses, had failed to understand him and that he had never been so humiliated in all of his days.[3]*

Men's underpants in the twentieth century seem to have reflected prevailing attitudes to the penis. The artificial penis enlargement, connoting the rank and status inherent in garments such as the codpiece, finds echoes in the image of male pop stars such as George Michael and Andrew Ridgeley of Eighties pop group Wham! who positioned shuttlecocks carefully down the front of tight white tennis shorts to create the same effect. But if men's underwear is about dick size what happens when women wear men's underwear?

ABOVE Tennis pro-turned-designer Bjorn Borg shows a catwalk collection of white cotton, androgynous underwear, which looks equally at home on both male and female bodies.

Take boxer shorts, which were originally issued to infantrymen for summer wear in America during the First World War. This specifically male undergarment underwent a massive revival in the 1980s when American retro was being heavily used in advertising. Levi's advertisements pioneered this particularly 1950s-inspired look in "Laundrette," which starred the model and erstwhile pop star Nick Kamen as the boy who strips down to his boxers. Kamen's cool good looks gave this type of underwear cult, and later mainstream, status. It was then appropriated by Madonna, who wore her boyfriend's boxer shorts in the 1985 film *Desperately Seeking Susan,* giving the undergarment credibility as women's wear. Quick to recognize a trend, Calvin Klein duly brought out a range of unisex jockey shorts for women.

Subversion was inherent in this look of mixed messages. There was no penis in these pants and they were referencing a masculine arena – sports. The sports field has always been seen as a place for the boys, and in the nineteenth century notions of Christian manliness meant that physicality and the muscled body acted as markers of male activity. As the home became increasingly feminized and men's work became concomitantly industrialized, participation in healthy outdoor sports was believed to be a necessity for the masculine man. Physical fitness was a masculine ideal and even now our most prominent male role models tend to be sportsmen – those who play to win. Wimps get sand kicked in their faces and participation is all, even if it is simply by being a spectator: sports bars are filled with hordes of excitable men cheering on their team as they watch the latest match on big screen television. However, as the

RIGHT In contrast, Hanro's underwear advertisement strictly demarcates the sexes: the men are active participants in the sports arena, the woman merely exposed as a decorative object.

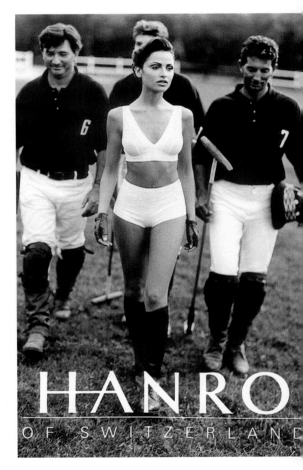

twentieth century progressed, women entered the world of physical culture in ever-increasing numbers. Their presence there today reflects freedom in all other areas of life – and that includes underwear.

Sportswomen of the early twentieth century had to suffer the physical restrictions of constructed underclothes in order to retain their status as "ladies" as their presence within competitive sports was not yet considered quite "respectable." Among the most notorious sportswomen of the time were lady cyclists who wore loose-fitting bloomers as outer garments. These bifurcated garments had caused consternation when they first appeared as undergarments in the 1850s. While undergoing a rest cure at a Swiss sanitarium, the American Amelia Bloomer had been inspired by the Turkish-type trousers worn by her friend Elizabeth Cady Stanton. She transformed the garment that had signified a sickly, passive femininity into a proto-feminist garment. The pioneering bloomer wearers came under a lot of flak – some women were even stoned.

Bifurcated garments were so solidly ensconced in the vocabulary of masculine dress that bloomers were not really accepted as undergarments until the end of the nineteenth century. The lady cyclists who wore them as overgarments at the beginning of the twentieth century presented such a shocking sight because the bloomers looked suspiciously like drawers even though they were made of coarse cloth. Cecil Saint Laurent writes, "at a time when clothes and underclothes enveloped a woman and veils, gloves and muffs were used to hide what little of her body escaped the dress, the sight of these cyclists in bloomers, gripping the saddle between their thighs aroused men violently."[4]

OPPOSITE Underpants come in all shapes and sizes. This pair are designed in a simple V-shape that makes reference to male styles and cuts. Illustration by Kareem Iliya.

ABOVE Patricia of Finland's bright blue vest and pants are the ultimate in easy underwear, with no tricky fastenings. The use of Lycra makes it simple to peel the duo on and off.

Early sportswomen who had no wish to court notoriety were compelled to conform to the rules of respectable underwear no matter how painful. Cultural historian Elizabeth Wilson writes of Betty Ryan, a Wimbledon tennis star before the First World War, who recalled that women's dressing rooms in English tennis clubs up to and during the First World War provided a rail near the fireplace on which the steel-boned corsets in which women played would be dried: "It was never a pretty sight, for most of them were blood-stained."[5]

As cultural attitudes to women and sport changed and women's athletic rather than reproductive function began to be acknowledged, manufacturers responded with more practical underwear. Developments commenced in 1938 with Dupont's invention of nylon, which led to easy care, drip dry underwear and sportswear. Lycra followed in 1950, a miraculous fabric by the same company comprised of a knit using two yarns: synthetic polyester or polyamide and elastic fiber or spandex. This new fabric technology did away with traditional fasteners, could be fused with other materials, such as cotton jersey, was resistant to perspiration, and could stretch four times its own length and still retain its shape.

Sportswomen began to ignore the traditionally "feminine" flouncy look when it came to their underwear – entering a masculine arena no longer necessarily meant they were compromising their femininity. Gussie Moran may have had to flash an overtly frilly pair of knickers designed by Teddy Tinling at Wimbledon in 1949 but by the 1970s it was OK for women to sweat rather

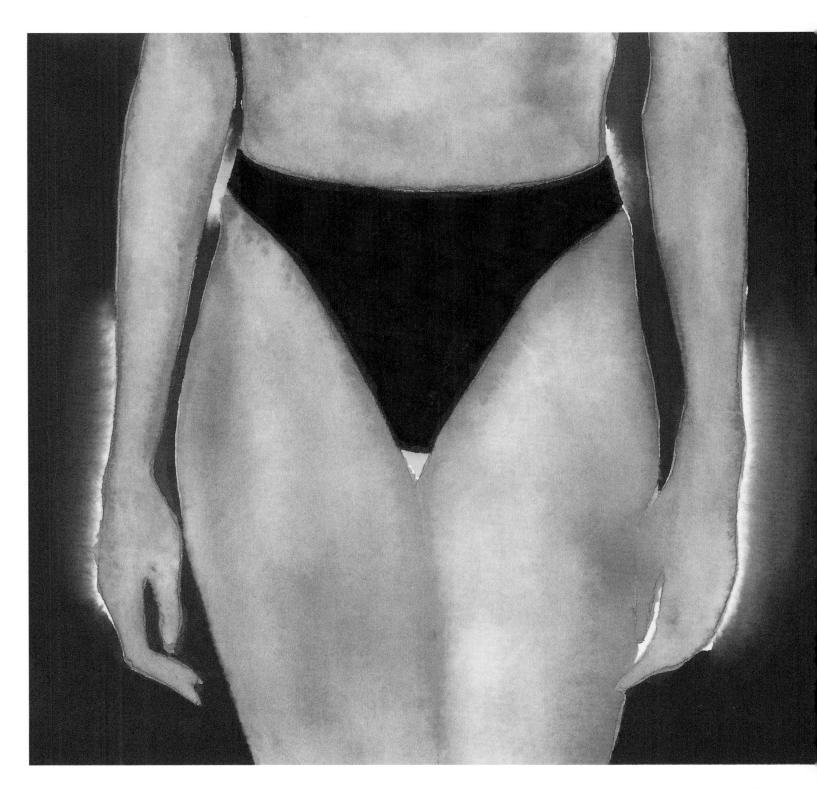

ABOVE Sloggi briefs are made of an almost magical combination of cotton and Lycra that clings closely and almost invisibly to the body – a simple solution to the visible panty line.

than just glow prettily on the sports field. The change came with the rise in women participating in exercise inspired by figures such as Jane Fonda and her range of work-out videos. Women went for the burn in dance-inspired leotards, footless tights and legwarmers, copying a look seen in many films and television productions including *Fame* (1980) and *Flashdance* (1983).

Original dancewear was bought from the Danskin company or from the more fashionable Pineapple label. Debbie Moore, who founded the eponymous dance studio in 1979, stated that "much of what I do is inspired by the stretchy clothing of dancers. I started designing originally because I couldn't find the right color or style."[6] The success of Moore's studio and products helped leggings reach a mass fashion market, which was also attained by the "body," a garment derived from the dancer's leotard and the Seventies body stocking. The body stocking, or body suit, was worn as part of the short-lived fad for roller-disco. Teamed with a pair of shorts or a ra ra skirt, the stretch body suit was acceptable as a perfect day-to-evening ensemble. Olivia Newton-John became a teenage icon in the 1978 film *Grease* when transformed from mousy schoolgirl into a diva in high heels, leather jacket and black body suit.

Tightly fitting exercise wear has developed into a legitimate mode for displaying the worked-out female body. The fashion historian Julian Robinson sees a sexual motive in its popularity.

The leotard shapes the waistline, rounds the hips, lifts the bust and
emphasizes the pubic area. This not only makes the wearer feel good
because of the slight pressure and friction on her clitoris, but makes her
look good as well because of her sexual glow – the same sexual glow
some girls achieve by wearing tight jeans and our ancestors achieved
a hundred years ago by wearing tightly laced corsets.[7]

His ideas notwithstanding it is clear that the "body," named because of its second skin nature, became one of the most manifest styles of the Eighties. Worn by many women workers as an alternative to the blouse under power suits, the artificial body operated as an idealized second skin over the inferior

BELOW A modern version of the ancient Roman *strophium*? Tommy Hilfiger plays with 1970s disco bunny fashion in this simple boob tube design, teamed with hipster jeans. The look has now become a standard silhouette.

OPPOSITE The first sports bra was invented by the American athlete Hinda Miller. Now a classic, the sports bra is designed without fasteners so it can simply be pulled over the head.

BELOW The span of what constitutes appropriate underwear for women is now so vast that a simple vest, such as this one by Joop, can exist alongside the plunging aesthetics of the Wonderbra.

biological body, ironing out its lumps and bumps as a result of the corset-like properties of Lycra. The shape and style of the "body" was perfected by Wolford, creating an even more streamlined form without side seams in 1992.

The description of this kind of underwear as "body controlling" is telling. Body maintenance has become the key to the successful lifestyle of the late twentieth century and discipline is all. The taboos around the intake of food and keeping the inner workings of the body pure through practices such as colonic irrigation have influenced underwear design, which today invokes a "naturalness" and "simplicity" to match the obsession with body engineering. (Ironically, this supposedly "natural" look runs concurrently with an emphasis on the artificial in the guise of the Wonderbra and other forms of erotic lingerie.) The sports bra is the ultimate in comfortable underwear, invented in 1977 by the runner Hinda Miller. Today sports bras are made of stretch fabric with no fasteners so that they can be pulled over the head easily, a direct response by designers to the needs of sportswomen. The sports bra has become a signifier of a "healthy lifestyle" rather than simply a garment worn by women athletes. Now a woman can use different forms of underwear to reflect her moods and actions. She changes from a sports bra with racing back and air vents for comfort at the gym into a cleavage-enhancing, black lace balconette at night in one easy move – multiple masquerades of femininity in our post-modern world.

RIGHT The Pineapple label was founded by the dancer Debbie Moore in 1979, and originally produced underwear inspired by the stretch clothing of dancers. Moore's body-conscious leotards formed an important part of the glamorous underwear revival which was being spearheaded by designers such as Janet Reger.

OPPOSITE Debbie Moore's leotard-inspired designs were prototypes of 1980s aerobics separates, which appear in their most utilitarian form in these classic designs by Hanro.

OPPOSITE Diesel, a company better known for its idiosyncratic marketing campaigns for jeans, expands into the underwear market with these simple pieces inspired by athletic wear. The advertising copy makes clear who is in control.

BELOW The origins of the "body" are made apparent in this ad campaign for Fogal. The model with her pale looks and ballerina's headband makes reference to classical dance, while her athletic pose is derived from gym culture.

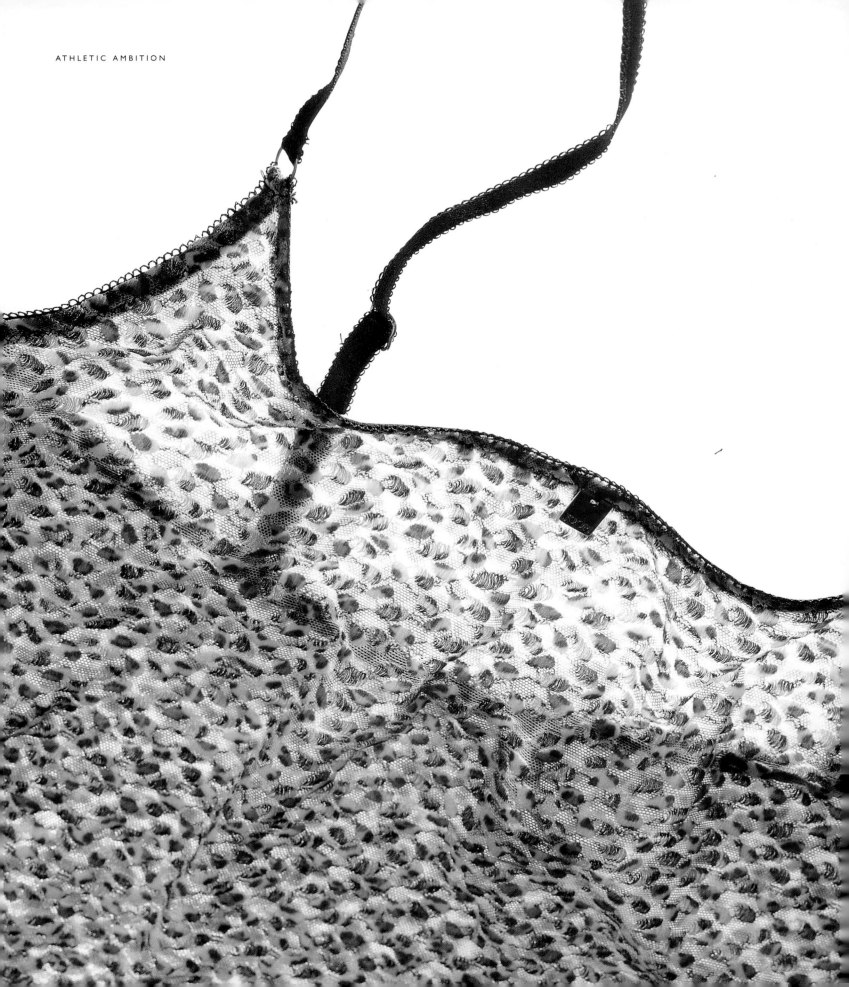

LEFT & BELOW Joop takes the utilitarian style of the athletic vest and briefs, and fuses it with the animal-print patterning associated with more traditionally sexy forms of feminine underwear to create a high-fashion combination of the sporty and decorative.

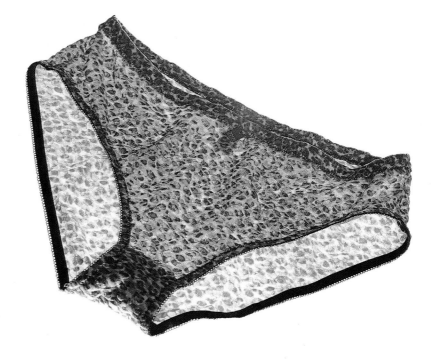

RIGHT Many women ignore the traditionally feminine, frilly look when it comes to their underwear and manufacturers have responded in kind producing much simpler styles. The dominance of the aesthetic of minimalism means underwear such as this signals that the wearer has good taste as well as a sense of practicality. This set is made to order by Jensens Dainties.

UNDER
DKNY
WEAR

OPPOSITE A woman in boxer shorts by DKNY, one of the most subversive of underwear images. The fly is redundant, there is no penis in these pants, thus our expectations are denied and the traditional signifiers of gendered dress destroyed.

RIGHT Armand Basi's underwear design is the ultimate minimalist statement – here a body-shaper which seems as much like a mummy's bandages as intimate apparel.

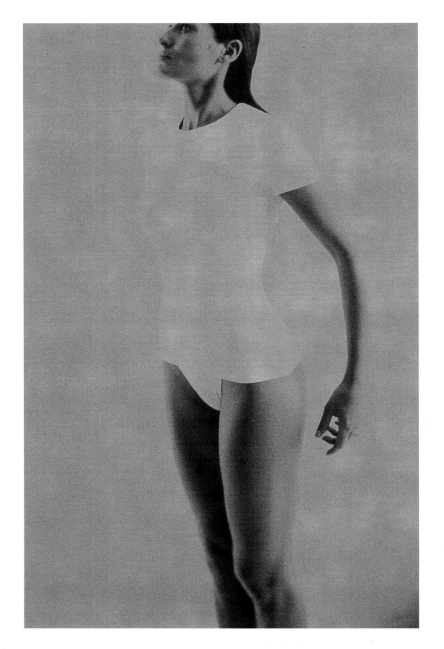

RIGHT In the nineteenth century, the writer Theodore Veblen saw extravagantly dressed women as parasites dependent on the financial support of men – condemned to be socially, economically, and psychologically dependent. This simple taxonomy of underwear shows how far women have come by the twenty-first century, no longer bearing the burdens of being the decorative sex. These cashmere vests by Brora combine the modern woman's passion for luxury with her desire for comfortable dress.

OPPOSITE Damart shows that thermal underwear can be sexy, too, using rose motifs to add interest to a functional garment.

BELOW & RIGHT Once demure, the dancer's leotard now sends different messages about the wearer depending on the cut and color employed. Fogal's navy leotard is classic in look, while Joop's scooped-out, flesh-toned version makes the associations with the skin beneath all too obvious. Thus the athletic connotations of dancewear are transmuted into a garment that makes the intentions of sexual display very clear.

LEFT An archetypal bra and briefs set by Debenhams. They are supportive yet decorative enough to wear under a transparent shirt – combining underwear and outerwear.

OPPOSITE This two-piece set by Patricia of Finland could be just at home on the beach, in a club, or a bedroom. Underwear is no longer to be whispered about, a taboo, but can be flaunted openly with pride. Photograph by Kira Gluschkoff.

Footnotes

INTRODUCTION

1. **Richard Martin and Harold Koda,** *Infra-Apparel* (New York: The Metropolitan Museum of Art, 1993), p.21.
2. **Alexander Lowen,** *In Defence of Modesty in Dimensions of Dress and Adornment: A Book of Readings,* (ed.) Lois M. Gurel and Marianne S. Beeson (Toronto: Kendall Hunt Publishing Company, 1979), p.146.
3. **Ted Polhemus,** *Bodystyles* (Luton: Lennard Publishing, 1988), p.114.
4. **Ted Polhemus,** *Bodystyles*, p.114.
5. **Richard Martin and Harold Koda,** *Infra-Apparel*, p.13.
6. **Valerie Steele,** *Fashion and Eroticism: Ideals of Feminine Beauty from the Victorian Era to the Jazz Age* (New York: Oxford University Press, 1985), p.16.

CHAPTER I: WAISTED WEAR

1. **Betty Kirke and Issey Miyake,** *Vionnet* (New York: Chronicle Books, 1998), p.104.
2. *Vogue Daily*, 11 March 1999 at http://www.vogue.co.uk
3. **Thorstein Veblen,** *The Theory of the Leisure Class* (London: George Allen and Unwin, 1949), p.182.
4. **Vivienne Westwood** quoted in Caroline Evans and Minna Thornton, *Women and Fashion: A New Look* (London: Quartet Books, 1989), p.189.
5. **Michael Bywater,** "Unhook before you leap," *The Guardian* (18 July 1999).
6. **Philippe Perrot,** "Les Dessus et les Dessous de la bourgeoisie," in Beatrice Fontanel, *Support and Seduction: A History of Corsets and Bras* (New York: Harry N. Abrams, 1998), p.54.
7. **Fontanel,** *Support and Seduction: A History of Corsets and Bras*, p.59.
8. Ibid.
9. **Alison Carter,** *Underwear: The Fashion History* (London: Batsford, 1992).
10. **Valerie Steele,** *Fashion and Eroticism; Ideals of Feminine Beauty from the Victorian Era to the Jazz Age* (New York, Oxford: Oxford

University Press, 1985).

11. David Kunzle, *Fashion and Fetishism: a Social History of the Corset and Tight-Lacing* (Totowa, New Jersey: Rowan and Littlefield, 1982), p. 29.

12. Misty at http://www.romantasy.com

13. Susan Faludi, *Backlash: The Undeclared War Against Women* (London: Chatto and Windus, 1992).

14. Helene Roberts, "The Exquisite Slave: The Role of Clothes in the Making of the Victorian Woman," *Sign* (Vol.2, no.3, Spring 1977).

15. Elizabeth Wilson, *Adorned in Dreams: Fashion and Modernity* (London: Virago, 1985), p.10.

16. Gayelord Hauser, *Look Younger, Live Longer* (London: Faber and Faber Ltd mcmli 1951), pp. 171-2.

17. Valerie Steele, *Fetish: Fashion, Sex and Power* (New York, Oxford: Oxford University Press, 1996), p.58.

18. Sigmund Freud, "Fetishism," *On Sexuality: Three Essays on the Theory of Sexuality and Other Works* (London: Penguin. 1977), p.352.

19. Louise J. Kaplan, *Female Perversions* (London: Penguin 1991), p.54.

20. Freud, "Fetishism," *On Sexuality: Three Essays on the Theory of Sexuality and Other Works*, pp.354-355.

21. Fontanel, *Support and Seduction: A History of Corsets and Bras*, p.74.

22. Havelock Ellis in Julian Robinson, *Body Packaging: a Guide to Human Sexual Display* (London: Guild Publishing, 1990), p.32.

23. Paula Sanchez at http://www.geocities.com

24. Mr Pearl in Steele, *Fetish: Fashion, Sex and Power*, p.83

25. Fakir Musafar in *Modern Primitives: An Investigation of Contemporary Adornment and Ritual* (USA: Re/Search Publications, 1989), p.29.

26. Ibid, p.31.

27. Ted Polhemus, *Streetstyle: From Sidewalk to Catwalk* (London: Thames and Hudson 1994), p.104.

28. Cathy Schwictenberg, *The Madonna Connection: Representational Politics, Subcultural Identities* (Colorado: Westview Press Inc., 1993), p.199.

29. Martin and Koda, *Infra-Apparel*, p.44.

30. Ibid.

CHAPTER 2: CLEAVAGE LINES

1. Elizabeth Haik, *Venus Envy: A History of Cosmetic Surgery*, (Baltimore: John Hopkins University, 1997), p.242.

2. Cecil Saint Laurent, *A History of Ladies Underwear* (London: Michael Joseph, 1968), p.10.

3. Beatrice Fontanel, *Support and Seduction: A History of Corsets and Bras* (New York: Harry N.Abrams, 1997), pp.20-21.

4. Beatrice Fontanel, *Support and Seduction: A History of Corsets and Bras*, p.68.

5. Peter Lewis, *The Fifties*, (London: William Heinemann Ltd, 1978), p.50.

6. Peter Lewis, *The Fifties*, p.53.

7. Karen Newman and Karen W. Bressler, *A Century of Style: Lingerie*, (London: Apple Press, 1998), p.55.

8. Elizabeth Haik, *Venus Envy: A History of Cosmetic Surgery*, p.243.

9. Elizabeth Haik, *Venus Envy: A History of Cosmetic Surgery*, p.244.

10. Germaine Greer, *The Female Eunuch* (London: Paladin, 1971), p.34.

11. Alison Carter, *Underwear. The Fashion History* (London: B.T Batsford Ltd., 1992), p.9.

12. Elizabeth Haik, *Venus Envy: A History of Cosmetic Surgery*, p.274.

13. Bibi van de Zee, "Learning Curves," *The Guardian* (Feb. 25, 1999).

14. Colin McDowell, *Dressed To Kill: Sex, Power and Clothes* (London: Hutchinson, 1992), p.177.

15. Jean-Paul Gaultier, interview with Richard Smith, *Gay Times* (January 1994), p.58.

16. Valerie Steele, *Fetish: Fashion, Sex and Power* (New York, Oxford University Press, 1996), p.134.

17. Susannah Baron, "Undercover Agents," *The Guardian* (Friday, 18 June 1999)

18. Hettie Judah, "Life after the Plunge," *The Guardian* (22 March 1999).

19. Beatrice Fontanel, *Support and Seduction: A History of Corsets and Bras*, p.144.

CHAPTER 3: HIP ZONE

1. Angela Carter, *Wise Children* (London: Chatto and Windus, 1991), p.43.

2. Rosemary Hawthorne, *Oh Knickers! A Brief History of Unmentionables*, (London: Bachman and Turner, 1985), p.65.

3. Cecil Saint Laurent, *The Great Book of Lingerie* (London: Academy Editions, 1986), p.65.

4. Ted Polhemus, *Bodystyles* (Luton, Lennard Books, 1988), p.118.

5. Alison Carter, *Underwear. The Fashion History* (London: Batsford, 1992), p.46.

6. Saint Laurent, *The Great Book of Lingerie*, p.113.

7. Clarel Brand, *Fetish* (London: Luxor Press, 1970), p.29.

8. *The Starr Report.* Referral to the United States House of Representatives pursuant to Title 28, US Code 595 (c)

9. Lawrence Langner, *The Importance of Wearing Clothes* (London: Constable and Co., 1959), p.235.

10. Langner, *The Importance of Wearing Clothes*, p.236.

11. J.C Flugel, *The Psychology of Clothes* (London: The Hogarth Press, 1930), p.66.

CHAPTER 4: BOUDOIR CHIC

1. http://www.starlingtech.com/quotes/qsearch.cgi

2. Susan Faludi, *Backlash: The Undeclared War Against Women* (London: Chatto and Windus, 1992), p.224.

3. Jennifer Craik, *The Face of Fashion: Cultural Studies in Fashion* (London, Routledge, 1984), p.121.

4. Octave Uzanne, in Valerie Steele, *Fashion and Eroticism : Ideals of Feminine Beauty from the Victorian Era to the Jazz Age* (New York: Oxford University Press, 1985), p.205.

5. Valerie Steele, *Fashion and Eroticism : Ideals of Feminine Beauty from the Victorian Era to the Jazz Age*, p.194.

6. Ibid.

7. Alison Carter, *Underwear: The Fashion History* (London: Batsford, 1992), p.98.

8. Alison Carter, *Underwear: The Fashion History*, p.96.

9. Karen Newman and Karen W. Bressler, *A Century of Style: Lingerie* (London: Apple Press, 1998), p.40.

10. Angela Carter, "The Bridled Sweeties" in *Nothing Sacred: Selected Writings*, (London: Virago, 1982), p.97.

11. Ibid.

12. http://www.cascadegrp

13. Louisa Young, "A Slip of a Thing" in *The Guardian* (Thurs, 30 Sept 1999).

14. Ibid.

15. "Notes from the Catwalk" in British *Vogue* (21 Jan 1999).

CHAPTER 5: ATHLETIC AMBITION

1. Leonore Davidoff and Catherine Hall, *Family Fortunes: Men and Women of the English Middle Class 1780-1850* (London, Hutchison, 1987), p.29.

2. Jennifer Craik, *The Face of Fashion: Cultural Studies in Fashion* (London, Routledge, 1984), p.137.

3. Harry Pearson, "Beware of Flying Underpants," *The Guardian* (Saturday, Jan 16, 1999).

4. Cecil Saint Laurent, *The Great Book of Lingerie* (London, Academy Editions, 1986), p.140.

5. Elizabeth Wilson, *Adorned in Dreams: Women, Fashion and Modernity* (London, Virago, 1984), p.99.

6. Karen Newman and Karen W. Bressler, *A Century of Style: Lingerie.* (London Apple Press, 1998), p.82.

7. Julian Robinson, *Body Packaging: A Guide to Human Sexual Display* (Los Angeles, Elysium Growth Press, 1999), p.176.

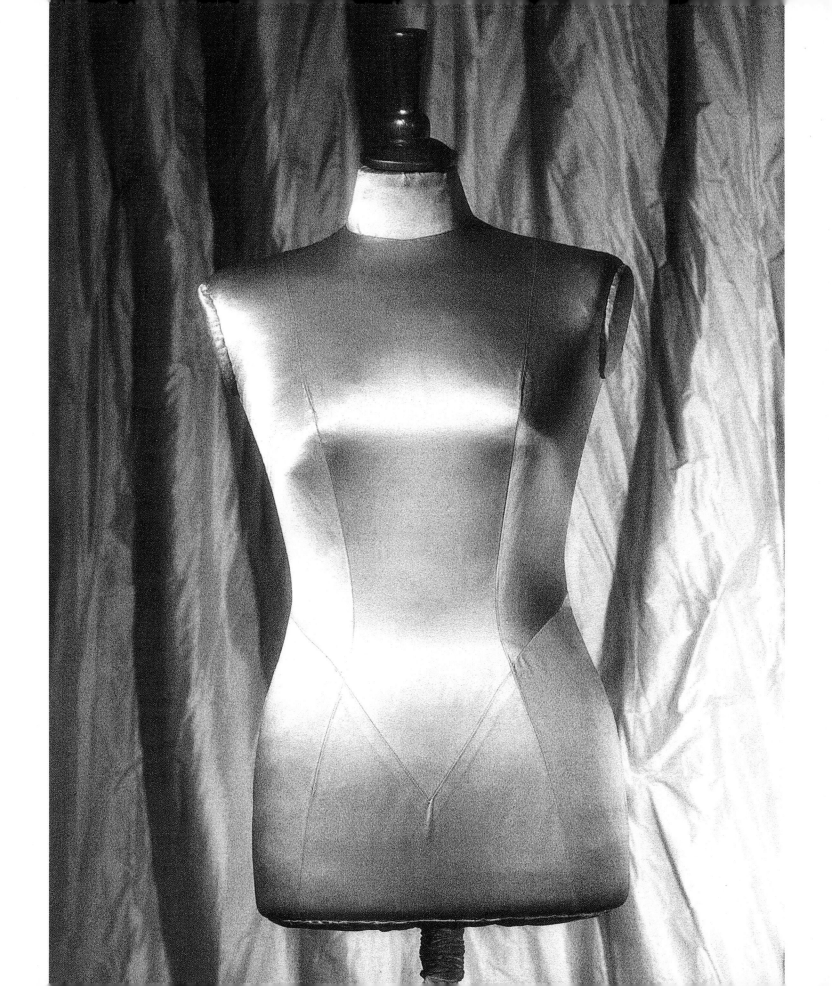

Picture Credits

ALESSANDRO DELL' ACQUA ph Stefan Sandonnini 66, 77, 149. ANN SUMMERS 13, 92. ARISTOC model Melanie Sykes 102, 118, 123. ARMAND BASI 177. BELLA FREUD ph Suresh Karadia 138. BJORN BORG 54, 160. BLUMARINE 127, 153. BRORA 178. CALVIN KLEIN ph Stephen Meisel, model Christy Turlington, courtesy United Talent Agency 76. CHANEL ph Karl Lagerfeld, model Brandi courtesy of Karin Models, S/S ready-to-wear collection 1994 45. CHARNOS 98. CHILA KUMARI BURMAN courtesy of Andrew Mummery Gallery 98. COLLETTE DINNIGAN ph Shane Martin 2. DAMART 104, 112. DEBENHAMS 83, 148, 182. DIESEL 170 Diesel Creative Team. DKNY 129, 176. FILA 167. FOGAL 99, 158, 171, 180. FREDERICK'S OF HOLLYWOOD 50, 59. FRED CORCORAN assistant: Dee Johnston, model: Sarah Cookson, make-up: Maria Comparetto; underwear courtesy of Sh! 34, 55, 81, 90, 100, 104, 122, 151; corsetry courtesy of Basia Zarzycka 39, 42, 43, 187; underwear courtesy of Beau Bras 84, 117; underwear courtesy of Joop 116, 150, 166, 172-3, 181; underwear by Divertimenti courtesy of Philippa Bradley Agency 128; underwear courtesy of Janet Reger 145; underwear courtesy of Jensens Dainties 174-5. FRENCH CONNECTION ph Oberto Gili 140. GEORGES RECH 159. GIRLY NYC ph Tom Schierlitz 101, ill Liz Pop 135, ph Susan San Giovanni 143. GOSSARD ph Liz McAulay 69. HANRO OF SWITZERLAND 82, 161, 169. HARRODS ARCHIVE (from *Harrods News*, 22 October 1923) 133. HULTON GETTY PICTURE LIBRARY ph Kurt Hutton 80, ph Fox Photos 93. JANET REGER 40, 112-13, 137, 142. JEAN CLAUDE JITROIS courtesy of Sloane Street, London, store 4. JEAN PAUL GAULTIER 72-3. JOHNNY DEWE MATTHEWS Tim Curry as Frankenferter in *The Rocky Horror Picture Show*. 24. JOSEPH 88. KAREEM ILIYA 110-11, 163. KAREN HATCH 89. KAREN MILLEN 147. KENZO 57, 64, 130. KNICKERBOX ph Willy Camden 27, 75, 114, 136, 139, 152, 157. LE BOURGET 96-7, 103, 119. LISELOTTE WATKINS Unit NYC 51. LIZA BRUCE 11. LUCY FITTER model Josephine Ruika courtesy of Storm 89. MARY QUANT 93, 95. MIU MIU 106-7. MOSCHINO F/W 88-89 collection 25. MUSEUM OF LONDON 18, 19, 20, 35. NINA RICCI 37, 65, 78, 79, 105. PATRICIA OF FINLAND ph Kira Gluschkoff 67, 162, 183. PINEAPPLE featuring Debbie Moore 168. PLAYTEX The One and Only Wonderbra 52, 71, 109; Lovable 85. PHOTOGRAPHERS' LIBRARY 23. RICHARD GRAY 28, 31, 32-33, 126, 131. SLOGGI 164. STEVE HIETT courtesy of HN magazine, clothing by Liza Bruce and Juicy 108. TANYA LING 6-7, 28, 141. TIM GROEN Unit NYC 134. TOMMY HILFIGER 165. TRIUMPH INTERNATIONAL 68. VANESSA BEECROFT VB26, 1997 Galleria Lia Rumma, Naples Italy ph Armin Linke 120-1, VB20 1996, Institute of Contemporary Art, Philadelphia, PA 189. VIRGIN RECORDS 10. WARNER BROS. RECORDS 36. WARNERS 56, 60, 70. WIT & WISDOM ph Karen Hatch 46-7, 146. WOLFORD ph Helmut Newton Copyright Wolford 1996-2000: 9, 17, 91, 115; ph Bruno Bisang 74.

acknowledgments

Both the publisher and author would like to thank the following for their generous assistance:

ALESSANDRO DELL' ACQUA *(Francesca)*, ANDREW MUMMERY, ANN SUMMERS *(Louise Hearn)*, ART PARTNER *(Candice Marks)*, ARMAND BASI *(Sarah Potter)*, BASIA ZARZYCKA *(Anna at Aurelia PR)*, BEAU BRAS, BELLA FREUD *(Emma McNiven at Modus PR)*, BLUMARINE *(Paola Ruffo, Lara Mazza)*, BJORN BORG *(Gavin Murphy)*, BRENNAN GRAYSON, CALVIN KLEIN INC. *(Kristen Vigrass)*, CAROLINE NEVILLE ASSOCIATES *(Lucy Hedderwicke)*, CHANEL *(Marika Genty, Cécile Goddet)*, CHARNOS *(Chris Hartley)*, CHILA KUMARI BURMAN, COLLETTE DINNIGAN *(Victoria Johns)*, DEBENHAMS *(Karin Huisman)*, DIESEL *(Sam Newman)*, FOGAL *(Mrs Oertli)*, FRED CORCORAN, FRENCH CONNECTION *(Lilli Anderson)*, FREDERICK'S OF HOLLYWOOD *(Jim Scott)*, GEORGE RECH *(Annie Demellier)*, GIRLY NYC *(Pamela Atwood)*, HANRO OF SWITZERLAND *(Debbie Missing)*, HELMUT NEWTON, I.P.I. SERVICES SPA *(Verde Visconti)*, JANET REGER, JEAN PAUL GAULTIER, JITROIS *(Flora Gandolfo)*, JOSEPH *(Christina Macmillan at Halpern Associates)*, JUDY BENNET PR *(Paul Bhari)*, KAREEM ILIYA, KAREN HATCH, KARIN MODELS *(Brandi, Ruth Malka)*, KENZO *(Pauline Lewis, Roy Barnes at Alba Associates)*, KNICKERBOX *(Philippa Gore)*, LAIRD BORRELLI, LE BOURGET *(Linda Istead)*, LISELOTTE WATKINS, LIZA BRUCE *(Antonia Grant)*, THE LONDON PR COMPANY *(Paula Fisher)*, LUCY FITTER, MARY QUANT *(Camilla Twigg)*, MINOUCHE FERECH *(Annette Weber)*, MOSCHINO *(Stefania Vismara, Helene Cadario)*, NICOLE WEBER COMMUNICATIONS *(Britta Kluth)*, PATRICIA OF FINLAND *(Marjukka Bruun)*, PHYLLIS WALTERS PR *(Phyllis Walters)*, PHILIPPA BRADLEY AGENCY *(Philippa Bradley)*, PINEAPPLE *(Trisha, Debbie Moore)*, PURPLE *(Jo Tutchener)*, QUANTUM PR *(Sarah Davis)*, RICHARD GRAY, SH! *(Kai, Sophie, Jo and Debbie)*, STEPHANIE CHURCHILL PR *(Chris Cudahy)*, STEPHEN MEISEL, STEVE HIETT *(Philippe Brutus at Julian Meijer Associates)*, STORM *(Gavin Boardman)*, TANYA LING, TASCO PUPLICK, TIM GROEN *(Unit NYC)*, TODD OLDHAM *(Jamey Edgerton)*, TOMMY HILFIGER *(Suzanna Muher)*, TRIUMPH INTERNATIONAL *(Sue Loder)*, UNITED TALENT AGENCY *(Christy Turlington, Lisa Jacobson)*, VANESSA BEECROFT, VIRGIN *(Imogen Hollingsworth)*, WAREHOUSE *(Lorraine Pringle)*, WOLFORD *(Alina Zimmerhäckel)*, YELLOW DOOR *(Christine Morgan)*.